NORMAN MAILER: QUICK-CHANGE ARTIST

NORMAN MAILER
QUICK-CHANGE ARTIST

JENNIFER BAILEY

First published 1979 by
THE MACMILLAN PRESS LTD
London and Basingstoke
Associated companies in Delhi
Dublin Hong Kong Johannesburg Lagos
Melbourne New York Singapore Tokyo

Printed and bound in Great Britain by
REDWOOD BURN LIMITED
Trowbridge & Esher

British Library Cataloguing in Publication Data

Bailey, Jennifer
    Norman Mailer, quick-change artist
    1. Mailer, Norman – Criticism and interpretation
    I. Title
    813'.5'4   PS3525.A4152Z/

    ISBN 0-333-24810-4

For David
and Brian

Contents

viii   *Contents*

Acknowledgements

The author and publishers wish to thank the following who have kindly given permission for the use of copyright material:

Jonathan Cape Ltd for the extracts from *Barbary Shore* (1951) by Norman Mailer;

André Deutsch Ltd for the extracts from *The Naked and the Dead* (1948), *The Deer Park* (1955), *Advertisements for Myself* (1959), *The Presidential Papers* (1963), *An American Dream* (1965) and *Cannibals and Christians* (1966) by Norman Mailer;

Grosset and Dunlap Inc for the extracts from *Marilyn* (1973) by Norman Mailer;

Scott Meredith Literary Agency Inc for the extracts from *Deaths for The Ladies* (1962), *Maidstone: A Mystery* (1971) and *St George and the Godfather* (1972) by Norman Mailer;

Scott Meredith Literary Agency Inc and Grove Press Inc for the extracts from *Genius and Lust: A Journey through the Major Writings of Henry Miller* (1976) by Norman Mailer;

Weidenfeld (Publishers) Ltd. for the extracts from *Why Are We in Vietnam?* (1967), *Miami And The Siege of Chicago* (1968), *The Armies of the Night* (1968), *A Fire on the Moon* (1970) and *The Prisoner of Sex* (1971) by Norman Mailer.

Every effort has been made to trace all the copyright-holders but, if any have been inadvertently overlooked, the publishers will be pleased to make the necessary arrangement at the first opportunity.

Introduction

One of the major obstacles to a proper understanding of Norman Mailer's work is his series of pronouncements on the nature of his ambitions. If these remarks are taken quite literally then Mailer's achievements can easily be distorted. Dotted throughout his writing since 1959, when *Advertisements for Myself* was published, is a thinly veiled longing to embody the conflicting currents of thought in the twentieth century just as Melville did in the nineteenth. The response to this has often been to regard Mailer's novels as noble but failed efforts and to settle for his journalism as a frequently brilliant but comparatively second-class literary activity. His forays into politics, poetry, biography, literary criticism, the theatre and film-making are then relegated to the amateur efforts of a versatile man. This kind of pigeonholing tends to miss the essentially innovatory nature of Mailer's talent.

In *The Armies of the Night* (1968), Robert Lowell makes the same mistake when he assures Mailer, ' "I really think you are the best journalist in America".' Mailer irritably replies, ' "Well, Cal, . . . there are days when I think of myself as being the best writer in America".'[1] The point is that throughout his career, Mailer has attempted to transgress and transform the boundaries between literary genres in order to realise and maintain a major premise first defined in *Advertisements for Myself*: 'one may even attempt to reshape reality in some small way with the "fiction" as a guide'.[2]

In order to see how a writer like Mailer engages with these polarities, it is useful to turn to the analysis by Richard Poirier, in his book *A World Elsewhere*, of the relationship between self and environment in the American imagination. Poirier considers that the categorisation of American writing into genres tends to obscure the more important issues. 'The crucial problem for the best American writers is to evade all such categorizations and to find a language that will at once express and protect states of consciousness that cannot adequately be defined by conventional formulations . . . .'[3] By means of a richly metaphorical language, Mailer has maintained the premise, formulated in *Advertisements for Myself*, that 'There is finally no way one can try to apprehend complex reality without a "fiction" '.(181)

Mailer declares his aesthetic artifice even as it is reaching for a reality that threatens it. But he also wants to demonstrably exercise a control over that reality—to 'reshape' it. The development of Mailer's use of metaphorical oppositions in his writing reflects a movement towards an effective appropriation of the external world in his radical 'fictions'. In his early novels, Mailer opposes politics and history[4] in order to distinguish between collective and individual power. But as yet, this individual power is seen to be impotent, even though General Cummings in *The Naked and the Dead* (1948) hints at its subversive possibilities: ' "politics have no more relation to history than moral codes have to the needs of any particular man" '.[5] Mickey Lovett, the narrator of *Barbary Shore* (1951) puts this notion into a literary context. His projected novel must give the duplicitous social reality a historical meaning. Yet this historical meaning is, as yet, uncertainly defined. In 'The White Negro' (1957), civilised history is opposed to the personal history, or the new nervous system of the existential hipster. The essay defends the individual's independent choice to act against a society of 'conformity and depression'.(271) To stress the force of this radical rebellion, the act is always described as violent in a murderous or sexual sense. Because these actions are socially subversive, the hipster is entering an unknown realm and creating a causality to his actions that is distinct from the causality of impersonal 'civilized history . . .'(270)

The status of the hipster's personal time or new nervous system, which is the precondition of this subversive action, is uncertainly figurative in the context of the essay. But in suggesting that the psychopath (and Mailer argues that the hipster possesses a psychopathic personality) seeks love that is 'Not love as the search for a mate, but love as the search for an orgasm more apocalyptic than the one which preceded it . . . ' (279), Mailer first develops a metaphor which describes the method by which the individual searches for an independent and therefore creative means of self-expression. By employing the sexual metaphor, Mailer can relinquish the term history as representing everything beyond the individual's control. The forces that threaten the creative act are found within a metaphor that is restricted to the creative life of one individual and by extension to Mailer himself. He is not forced to oscillate confusedly between literal and figurative terms of reference in order to incorporate the world into his writing. Any sexual activity that prevents conception undermines the individual's selfhood. Masturbation, buggery and contraception are therefore condemned. Mailer reiterates his views from the publication of *The Presidential Papers* (1963) onwards, while the sexual activities of Sergius O'Shaugnessy in 'The Time of Her Time' and Stephen Rojack in *An American Dream* (1965) demonstrate these principles.

Mailer simultaneously developed another metaphorical opposition which similarly described the struggling precariousness of the individual's creativity. Although the notion of the hipster was the source of this opposition, Mailer only amplified it in a subsequent interview with Richard Stern, given in 1958 (reprinted in *Advertisements for Myself*):

And I think there is one single burning pinpoint of the vision in Hip: it's that God is in danger of dying. In my very limited knowledge of theology, this never really has been expressed before. I believe Hip conceives of Man's fate being tied up with God's fate. God is no longer all-powerful. (308–9)

This enables Mailer to go on to suggest that when the hipster takes drugs, for example, 'in draining the substance of God he's exhausting Him, so that the drug-taker may be indulging an extraordinarily evil act at the instant he is filled with the feeling that he is full of God and good and a beautiful mystic'. (310) As with his sexual metaphor, Mailer is trying to define metaphysical entities within the individual in order that oppressive external forces can be incorporated into his fiction.

Until *Advertisements for Myself*, Mailer confined these metaphysical metaphors to the context of the rebellious hipster. But in a speech delivered on Vietnam Day in 1965 and reprinted in *Cannibals and Christians* (1966), Mailer argues that anyone is 'a member of a minority group if he contains two opposed notions of himself at the same time . . . as both exceptional and insignificant, marvellous and awful, good and evil'.[6] The advantage of giving his metaphors a universal psychological relevance is that Mailer can successfully employ them in his works of fictional reporting as well as in his two novels written at this time: *An American Dream* and *Why Are We in Vietnam?* (1967). An image in the anti-Vietnam speech of 'the ego in

perpetual transit from the tower to the dungeon and back again'
(101) describes the satirised archetypal quest form of *An American
Dream*, but it also leads Mailer towards the kind of oppositions he
defines in his work at the end of the 1960s.

If Mailer's metaphorical oppositions attempt to stress the
precariousness of artistic creativity, then the greatest threat will
come from literal and therefore uncontrolled reality. In his sexual
and metaphysical metaphors, Mailer transforms this literal and
almost always oppressive reality into a dialectical entity within the
individual. *The Armies of the Night, Miami and the Siege of Chicago*
(1968) and Mailer's film *Maidstone* (1970), successfully incorporate
non-fictional realms without there being any threat to their
aesthetic structure. In *The Armies of the Night*, Mailer reintroduces
the term 'history' to signify the collective reality that modifies the
individual vision of his protagonist. In the essay written about his
film, *Maidstone: A Mystery* (1971), this collective reality is the force
that ambiguously blurs the acted fiction of the film. But *Miami and
the Siege of Chicago* is narrated by a reporter who is professionally
obliged to observe and record the events he witnesses.

The function of Mailer's metaphors, however, is not just to
extend the boundaries of fiction, but also explicitly to demonstrate
that it can interpret the world in a social, political and cultural
sense. Mailer's writing begins successfully to fulfil that claim when
he controls the form of his fiction which records the struggling
dialectical activity of his protagonist. Norman Mailer is, in this
sense, an artist whose formal control distinguishes him from the
vulnerable artist figures in his fiction.

Ihab Hassan's theory of radical irony, which he introduces and
defines in the prologue to his book, *The Literature of Silence*,
illuminates the nature of Mailer's achievement. Hassan initially
advances the proposition that certain contemporary writers acknowledge what critics tend to ignore by providing the mirror-
images of outrage and apocalypse 'that contain something vital and
dangerous in our experience'.[7] At the centre of these extreme
responses is a silence which Hassan describes 'as the metaphor of a
new attitude that literature has chosen to adopt toward itself'.[8] This
new attitude is one which 'compels the author to deprecate and
even to spurn his activity'.[9] Hassan's description of the silence which
is achieved in this kind of literature through radical irony describes
the function of Mailer's protagonists in his work after *Advertisements
for Myself*. Hassan explains that radical irony is 'a term I apply to

any statement that contains its own ironic denial'.[10] When this technique is practised by fiction writers, the result is 'the paradox of art employing art to deny itself [which] is rooted in the power of human consciousness to view itself both as subject and object'.[11] All of Mailer's protagonists after 1959 possess this power, so that the impulse to create is always fought for because it can only be expressed in the context of those forces that threaten it.

It is possible, however, to trace the development of these ideas in Mailer's fiction written before *Advertisements for Myself*. In his first three novels—*The Naked and the Dead, Barbary Shore* and *The Deer Park* (1955)—Mailer explores the discrepancy that seems to exist between the individual and the world; the discrepancy between moral choice and political expediency or between the artist and corrupt oppressive external forces. Mailer tries to resolve this dilemma by developing the idea that identity is always a fiction in so far as it depends upon a constantly changing milieu for its definition. He wanted, though, to explore the practical connotations of this theory, to synthesise fictional and literal frames of reference. Yet no matter how much the writer may want his fictional world to reflect the real one, it remains a created object. *Advertisements for Myself* was a breakthrough in that Mailer made himself a protagonist whose identity is a composite of roles that are triggered off by a variety of contexts both autobiographical and cultural. He simultaneously discovered that the reactions of a public audience was a necessary prerequisite for this form of writing. It was not an established literary reputation that he wanted, but a notoriety. Mailer admires and respects the talents of Saul Bellow, for example, but he observes, in *Cannibals and Christians*, that while Bellow writes classics, they are not major novels 'which is a way of saying . . . he is not too likely to seize the temper of our time and turn it'.(158)

Mailer consolidated his achievements when he discovered that the nature of improvised acting was analogous to his radical ideas on fiction. John Kennedy in 'The Superman Comes to the Supermarket'[12] is defined by Mailer as both a serious politician and a great box-office actor. Since Mailer characterises himself as an appreciative if bewildered spectator, his shifting perceptions dictate the actor's series of roles on the stage (in this case, a literal one, since the occasion is the 1960 Democratic National Convention in Los Angeles). In so doing, Mailer presents Kennedy as the personification of an ambiguous social reality.

From this, it was a short step to Mailer being both actor and audience in the performances of his personae which dominate his fictional reporting[13] published in the late 1960s. The characters in *An American Dream* and *Why Are We in Vietnam?* are conceived in the same way as these personae. They shift roles, voices and points of view with the same rapidity and possess only the most conventional of physical embodiments in order that they might be mockingly dismembered by one of their many roles. Mailer has previously been underrated or ignored as a film director, yet the process of filming and the theories that he evolved from this process illuminate a period of prodigious activity.

Although it may now be possible to detect an impending creative impasse in Mailer's fiction of the shifting identity, this kind of radical fictionalising, first defined in *Advertisements for Myself*, still constitutes the foundation on which his unique talent rests.

To write about myself is to send my style through a circus of variations and postures, a fireworks of virtuosity designed to achieve . . . I do not even know what. Leave it that I became an actor, a quick-change artist, as if I believe I can trap the Prince of Truth in the act of switching a style. (17–18)

1 'The Peculiar Megalomania of a Young Writer'

In the prefatory Advertisement to an early story, 'A Calculus at Heaven' (1944), Norman Mailer wrote: 'I think its tone gives away the peculiar megalomania of a young writer who is determined to become an important writer.'(26) Although the choice of subject— the war between the Americans and Japanese in the Pacific—is an obvious one for 1942, Mailer is not, like his predecessors, simply protesting against the organisation of war that propels men helplessly toward their death. Unlike Hemingway, who depicts violence as the manifestation of an incomprehensible force, Mailer believed it to be individually satisfying: 'life and death and violent action were the fundamentals, and he would find no lie there.'(47) Unlike the characters in John Dos Passos' novel, *USA*, who are deterministically manipulated by destructive social forces, Mailer attempts to show that his characters are being shaped, as they approach death, by forces within themselves.

The action of the story covers the retreat of five men from a heavy Japanese attack into a fortressed house, the death of three of them and the calm anticipation of certain death on the part of the remaining two. Because the story is structured by the internal monologues of the five men, because they are situated in a confined space, the war with the Japanese takes on a slightly unreal aspect. We are confronted, instead, with five internal battles of which the Pacific War represents a final climactic metaphor. Father Meary fights the dishonesty of his religious vocation, Da Lucci viciously attacks the injustice of his harsh upbringing. Both these men are afraid because they are cowards in actual warfare. By contrast, Jewboy Wexler transfers his skill and love for a football game into the actual situation and so is able courageously to undertake a reconnaissance. Rice, the Indian, understands his stoicism in facing death in terms of his long experience with whores: 'he was gonna get his' just as the whore had told him 'some guys are born to go to whorehouses.'(63)

The story's principal character, Captain Bowen Hilliard, is attempting to discover a fundamental truth in the violent action of the Pacific War, that his failed marriage and compromised career have denied him. He believes, along with the philosopher Malraux 'that all that men are willing to die for tends to justify their fate by giving it a foundation in dignity.'(39) At first, Hilliard believes that he can break out of the impotent style of his frustrated radicalism though violent action and death, which will give the self the dignity to which Malraux refers. After the sudden and casual death of the courageous Wexler, he realises the flaw in that theory. The ecstasy of death can only be felt after the experience: 'emotion could only come from the connotations of experience, and not from the experience itself.'(57) Simply as an objective fact, death, like war, is meaningless; it needs the person who experiences it to select the important connotations of the experience from the context of that experience. Otherwise it is an impotent fact without a form.

Since his death is an inevitability, Hilliard considers an alternative to the practical fulfilment of the dignity that Malraux advocates. One can die for one's country, although Hilliard makes an interesting distinction in this notion. The word 'America' deserves only hatred and contempt. As a country, it offers a tenuous hope 'that something would come out of the country, and that it wouldn't go hard and selfish as it always had before.'(60) It is significant, though, that the only reviewer who had recognised the key sentence in Hilliard's book *The Artist in Transit Inglorious*, had rejected it as 'rot': 'To die in terms of a subsequent humanity is a form of emotional sophistication that may be achieved only by the people of that nation which puts its philosophy in action.'(61)

Bowen Hilliard fails then in his individual rebellion against 'style', 'the word America' and its 'Calculus at Heaven'. Despite his incipient nobility, despite Malraux's call for human dignity in death, there is no alternative to be found in the active world, because there is nothing to die for. Although Mailer obviously has some scorn for a man who would scream platitudes on Munch, Beckmann and Marin and who needs a war to propel him into action, he identifies with Bowen Hilliard's radicalism. In the prefatory Advertisement, he remembers Edwin Seaver, who accepted the story for publication, asking him '"You admire Malraux greatly?"', to which Mailer rejoined '"I'd like to be another Malraux"'.(26) Mailer however, can see no way of implementing the word, the theory, the ideological conviction in a society which is, despite his contempt and distrust, obviously important to him. Meary, Da Lucci, Wexler and Rice—the Irish, Italian, Jew and Indian—are a microcosm of American society. The fact that the men die pointlessly regardless of their courage or cowardice, the fact that it is unclear as to the extent that courage or cowardice is the result of social conditioning or individual choice, demonstrates Mailer's inability to find a practical dimension for his ideological convictions.

Nevertheless, in his first, enormously successful novel, *The Naked and the Dead*, Mailer maintained both his ideological drive and his determination that his personal vision should elevate his stature in the eyes of his country. His ambition was to 'clarify a nation's vision of itself'.(26) It was not sufficient to write a good novel; it had to be recognised as such by the reading public. When Steven Marcus, in the *Paris Review* interview given in 1967, quoted Faulkner as saying '"nothing can injure a man's writing if he's a first-rate writer"', Mailer violently rejected the remark as '"asinine . . ."'.(256)

The Naked and the Dead is preoccupied on one level with the confrontation between Fascism and liberalism, the outcome of which is a foreboding of the domination of the Right in response to the challenge of America's postwar dilemma. Diana Trilling argues that during Mailer's early writing career 'his novelist's mind is peculiarly violable by idea, even by ideology'.[1] Trilling is partially correct. But what she does not discern is that Mailer is simultaneously attempting, in *The Naked and the Dead*, to transform the determinism of these political and social forces into forces that are created and controlled by the individual. The action of *The Naked and the Dead* takes place on a Pacific Island called Anopopei, which is invaded by General Cummings and his troops in order to attack the Japanese garrison under General Tayaku and breach their defence beyond the Tayaku line. Combat action is principally focused upon a small reconnaissance platoon under the command of Sergeant Croft. Mailer juxtaposes the insufferable hardships of these men living in the tropical jungle with the relative comfort of the officer's camp. Death in combat with the Japanese is shockingly present in, for example, the agonised fear of Croft as the enemy swarm across the river under the cover of night, or the pathos of the minutely described long-dead Japanese bodies among which Croft's platoon drunkenly wander in search of loot. But the fight for survival takes place principally within the self. Existence on the island is felt most crucially, not in terms of staying alive or dying but of dominating or being dominated. The battles with the most at stake are to be found in the locking of wills of Red Valsen and Sergeant Croft, the defence of Goldstein's Jewish integrity against the antisemitism of the platoon, the struggle for dominance between the Fascist General Cummings and the liberal Lieutenant Hearn, or the conflict between Lieutenant Hearn and Sergeant Croft for effective leadership over the troops while climbing Mount Anaka.

It is in the confrontation between Cummings and Hearn that the novel's central thesis is presented; their exchange of ideas and conflict of emotions are the means by which the other confrontations are assessed. Hearn is a naive and uncompromising idealist, whose theoretical hope is that history will cyclically produce '"certain great ethical ideas"'.(153) But he realises that while he is impotently generalising about an abstract set of principles centred around a woolly notion that good must eventually triumph, Cummings eschews conventional morality in an attempt to gain complete control and dominance over the world in which he moves. Hearn gloomily admits to himself that postwar America will belong to men like Cummings: 'The League of Ominipotent Men'.(334) There is nothing to offer in opposition except to 'sit back and wait for the Fascists to louse it up'.(494) Mailer is confirming the ineffectiveness of the liberal ideology when Hearn is suddenly killed after deciding to give up his officer's commission on returning from the patrol through the Watamai Mountains. Croft is prepared to sacrifice the life of Hearn in his single-minded ambition to climb Mount Anaka. Although Croft and Cummings never meet, the two men are identical in the unscrupulousness with which they attempt to eliminate any obstacle to their naked ambition.

The meaning of Cummings' implicit equation of 'history' with the needs of the particular man is to be found in his contemptuous demonstrations of his power to Hearn. Cummings teaches Hearn that '"The fact that you're holding a gun and the other man is not is no accident. It's a product of everything you've achieved, it assumes that if you're . . . you're aware enough, you have the gun when you need it".'(73) This awareness suggests Cummings' belief that history can be converted into an exclusively personal force by the individual which will always place him in a position of superiority over men like Hearn, who put their faith in a notion of history as a cyclical machine. In their final confrontation, Hearn has ground a cigarette butt on the floor of Cummings' scrupulously neat tent in a frustrated gesture of defiance. Before humiliating Hearn, the General points out, '"It's not an accident that I have this power. Nor is it that you're in a situation like this. If you'd been more aware, you wouldn't have thrown down that cigarette".'(278) This remark is the culmination of an exchange between the two men on the nature of warfare. Hearn's ideas are vague; his guarded liberalism prompts him to an outright condemnation of Fascism as it applied to Nazi Germany because, as Cummings suspects, Hearn is afraid of the attraction it secretly holds for him. But Cummings confronts Hearn's fears by redefining Fascism in terms of man's innate power to change American society after Hitler's Germany has been defeated.

> Historically the purpose of this war is to translate America's potential into kinetic energy. The concept of fascism, far sounder than communism if you consider it, for it's grounded firmly in men's actual natures, merely started in the wrong country, in a country which did not have enough intrinsic potential power to develop completely.(275)

There is an incident early in the novel which parallels this exchange between Cummings and Hearn. A young private, Hennessey, is killed by a piece of shrapnel when the troops first invade Anopopei. Two men are particularly moved by this event. Both Red Valsen and Croft have forebodings of Hennessey's death. Valsen is moved to feel compassion for the young private because he follows the rule book so carefully. Like Hearn, who feels that America may fight Fascism only to adopt it after Germany has been defeated, Valsen knows that Hennessey is a loser because 'he was the kind of kid who would put away money for marriage before he even had a girl. It was what you got for following the rule book.'(16) While Croft also watches Hennessey's preparations for battle with the thought 'That boy is too careful . . . ' (29), he is stirred by the powerful conviction that '"Hennessey's going to get killed today"'.(ibid) Although he is disgusted with himself for feeling unsure as to whether this emotion can shape events, 'His disgust came because he felt he could not trust such emotions, rather than from any conviction that they had no meaning at all.'(ibid) Because Valsen has himself quietly admitted that he, unlike Hennessey, has jettisoned 'every gimcrack in his life',(16) he is appalled at the latter's death. 'It gave Red a moment of awe and panic as if someone, something, had been watching over their shoulder that night and laughing. There was a pattern where there shouldn't be one.'(37) Like Hearn, he is afraid to admit the power within himself that is secretly attracted to destroying the rule book. Croft, like Cummings, revels in his power: 'Hennessey's death had opened to Croft vistas of such omnipotence that he was afraid to consider it directly. All day the fact hovered about his head, tantalizing him with odd dreams and portents of power.'(38)

To Cummings and Croft, historical forces can be converted to individual power. The individual understands and controls the pattern of power when he '"achieves God"'.(277) As Cummings explains, man must maintain and act upon the belief with which he is born, which is that the universe is the limit of his senses: '"Man's deepest urge is omnipotence"'.(ibid) Croft's instinctive version of the same conviction is 'I HATE EVERYTHING WHICH IS NOT IN MYSELF'.(141) In terms of this scale of values, Hearn and Valsen are contemptible, not because they lack this omnipotent urge but because they are unable to come to terms with the fact that they possess it. Principally, Cummings, Croft, Hearn and Valsen are all alike in their urge to dominate; a fact which both Hearn and Valsen disgustedly recognise—Hearn in his relationship with Cummings and Valsen with the men in the platoon. As Hilliard reflects:

> If they had believed in something outside themselves, it would have been all right, but everything they had been told for the first twenty years of their lives had become on examination a piece of disjunctivity. The form and the matter had not coincided. So that having no end for their life, they had tried to get by on style.(47)

The casual death of Jewboy Wexler teaches Hilliard that the style of this jealously safeguarded integrity is hopelessly insufficient. 'Too late, it seemed to him ridiculously clear that emotion could only come from the connotations of experience, and not from the experience itself'.(57) Similarly, after Cummings has forced Hearn to pick up the cigarette off the floor of his tent, the latter feels a sense of shocking violation. Up till then, Hearn's working guide has been '"The only thing to do is to get by on style"'',(280) which is 'to let no one in any ultimate issue ever violate your integrity . . .' (ibid), which of course Cummings has just done. Like Hilliard, he is forced to acknowledge the connotations of the experience that are external to himself, and it plunges him into desperate confusion: 'He would have to react or die, effectively, and for one of the few times in his life he was quite uncertain of his own ability. It was impossible; he would have to do something, and he had no idea what to do'.(ibid)

The style that fails Hilliard and Hearn is quite plainly not the style that shapes the characters of Croft and Cummings. Croft is a competent platoon leader; he has a flexible, supple, adaptable style of action, which enables him to lead the men under his command up the hostile slopes of Mount Anaka. Yet despite their attempts to control the world around them, both Croft and Cummings fail. After Cummings' victory over Hearn in his tent, the latter issues a parting shot: ' "Short of bringing every man in the outfit, all six thousand of them, and letting them pick up your cigarettes, how are you going to impress them?" '(279) It finds its mark, because, as Cummings reflects after Hearn's departure, 'Hearn he had been able to crush, any single man he could manage, but the sum of them was different still, resisted him still'.(ibid) Cummings is forced to remain the inadequate theorist, 'playing with words . . .',(481) because he has reached the impossible dimensions of a megalomaniac. He tries to reduce the order of existence to a single curve, and although he knows this is a meaningless conceit, the longing remains: 'It was all there if only he could grasp it. To mold . . . mold the curve'.(482)

What Cummings has described, Croft illustrates on the slopes of Mount Anaka. Croft is not content just to do his job well, but is determined to reduce the men in the platoon to components of his will, once the mission proves to be agonisingly difficult to execute. The limits to Cummings' and Croft's tyrannical ambitions are proved in an absurd fashion. The American victory on Anopopei is apparently engineered by the bewildered and foolish Major Dalleson, although, as Cummings admits, 'it had been accomplished by a random play of vulgar good luck larded into a casual net of factors too large, too vague, for him to comprehend'.(602) The platoon and Croft retreat in panic down Mount Anaka, pursued by a swarm of angry hornets. Referring to the defeat of Cummings, Tony Tanner argues that 'the controller of the island is himself controlled in unfathomable ways . . .'.[2] But, in fact, Cummings and Croft are defeated because they have extended their individual power into impossible realms far beyond the connotations of their own experience, and so inevitably, and foolishly, come to grief.

In order for Mailer to demonstrate the ambitions and subsequent failure of Croft's and Cummings' notions upon individual power, he found it necessary to isolate his fictional setting from a recognisable social context. In his first prefatory Advertisement, Mailer explains that one of the reasons for choosing to write about the war in the Pacific rather than Europe was that 'you don't have to have a feeling for the culture of Europe and the collision of America upon it. To try a major novel about the last war in Europe without a sense of the past is to fail in the worst way—as an over-ambitious and opportunistic slick.'(26) And, in fact, the war on Anopopei is, like the war in 'A Calculus at Heaven', an abstraction, despite the palpable presence of death in the novel. In his use of Cummings' communiqués with Washington, Mailer pays lip-service to the world outside his fictional one. He does this in order to show that American social forces are ultimately irrelevant to the internal tensions on his fictional island. The map of Anopopei on the title page with its scale and labelling stresses both the concreteness and complete isolation of the novel's setting. The Pacific Ocean is vast and we have no idea of the island's location. Despite the fact that, as Diana Trilling observed, *The Naked and the Dead* displays a 'loyal delight in physical truth'[3] unequalled in *Barbary Shore* or *The Deer Park*, it is the most uncompromisingly imaginative of Mailer's early novels with regard to its setting. Hearn realises, as he is meditating upon the uniqueness of Cumming's power, that 'the General might even have been silly if it were not for the fact that here on this island he controlled everything. It gave a base to whatever he said'. Other men thought like him but their magnetism was lost to them in 'the busy complex mangle, the choked vacuum of American life'.(75) When Hearn has the honesty to admit his affinity with the man he loathes, he does so by disregarding both of their 'environmental trappings . . .'.(335) Through Cummings, who places him in command of the reconnaissance platoon on their expedition through the Watamai Mountains, he enjoys the desire to lead, to move men that is almost sexual in its ecstasy. In the heat of that basic lust, 'he was just another Croft'.(489)

Juxtaposed with this explicit disregard of 'environmental trappings' is a pervasive element of determinism. While Croft and Cummings are exponents of control over the wheel of existence, that provides an understanding of the order in death as well as in life, the structure of the novel with its 'Time Machine' sections begs the question as to the importance of the men's environment in shaping their characters. It is in these sections that America, the real world with its historical, social and political concomitants, intrudes in an uncompromising manner.

It is certainly possible to see the personalities of the novel's protagonists simply as the end product of certain ethnic or social backgrounds, yet Mailer attempts to transform and thereby vitiate the deterministic social forces that press upon his characters through the 'Time Machine' sections. He places upon his island a symbolic criterion by which the men may be judged in their potential ability to manipulate and control these social forces. Mount Anaka is the geographical centre of Anopopei and the symbolic centre of *The Naked and the Dead*. From the sea, the mountain dominates the landscape, and its size reduces, in more than just a physical sense, the battle between the American and Japanese armies. The men are trapped in the close, fetid, overcast jungle, while the mountain, made of another material, invisibly towers over them, independent of this claustrophobic and oppressive vegetation. When Cummings conceives of the daring plan to attack the Japanese Toyaku Line from the rear, it falls to Croft and his platoon, under the leadership of Hearn, to climb Mount Anaka, which is their principal obstacle in this mission.

As the mountain fills the sight of the men, both literally and emotionally, it shapes their characters. Viewing it from a distance, the mountain is imaged, by the authorical voice, as 'wise, powerful, and terrifying in its size'. Then Gallagher stares at it 'caught by a sense of beauty he could not express', because it represents a 'vision he always held of something finer and neater and more beautiful than the moil in which he lived . . . '. Red Valsen 'felt only gloom, and a vague harassment'.(378) As the men approach nearer to the mountain and finally move on to its slopes, they are forced to recognise that these emotions are pushing their characters into a climactic situation. Croft feels 'a crude ecstasy', Hearn is filled with awe and fear because 'It was too immense, too powerful'.(420) As the men approach the summit, the mountain finally seems endowed with intelligent life. To Croft, it is 'a human thing'(543) while to the rest of the platoon, worn by Croft's commands, the stairway of rocks 'became alive, personalized, it seemed to mock and deceive them at every step, resist them with every malign rock'.(590) But the very nature of the mountain resists the assault made upon it. Because Croft and Cummings cannot admit the distinction between being master of their experiences and the forces that shape them, and the urge to shape the experiences of others, the mountain has demonstrated this limit to them. Croft's last view confirms Mount Anaka's inviolate, pure remoteness and, in the light of the failure of

Cummings' mission, the latter's intuition that 'the mountain and he understood each other. Both of them, from necessity, were bleak and alone, commanding the heights'(475) is a foolish self-deception.

The problem with this symbol, however, is that although it provides a criterion for assessing the longings and ambitions of Croft, Cummings, Hearn and the platoon, it does not satisfactorily displace the social forces it is intended to transform. The patrol sit on the boat after their mission is cut short, faced with the fact that 'they were still on the treadmill; the misery, the ennui, the dislocated horror . . . Things would happen and time would pass, but there was no hope, no anticipation. There would be nothing but the deep cloudly dejection that overcast everything'.(593–94) The gloom of the men might conceivably be the gloom of Mailer, because American social forces and the forces on Anopopei are so clearly mutually exclusive. Mailer is searching for a means in his novels through which he can portray the history of the particular man which reflects and transforms the history of the social forces that surround him.

This is the theme of Mailer's second novel *Barbary Shore*. In the prefatory Advertisement to printed extracts from the novel, Mailer explains that not only had he to face the challenge presented by the enormous success of his earlier book, but the fact that 'my past had become empty as a theme'. He must 'write about an imaginary future . . . from the bombarded cellars of my unconscious . . . '.(87) Accordingly, his narrator, Mickey Lovett, is a man deprived of a past and therefore a future, visited by uncertain memories of war, but propelled by a driving ambition to write a novel. As *Barbary Shore* opens, he describes a fantasy that constantly recurs: a traveller returning from a trip and anxious to reach home, discovers that the city in which he lives has grown strange, unfamiliar. He concludes that he is dreaming, that the cab in which he is travelling and the city which he sees are imaginary. 'I shout at him. You are wrong, I cry, although he does not hear me; this city is the real city, the material city, and your vehicle is history.'[4] Mailer is defining the responsibility of the writer in this image. The novel is the vehicle which appropriates historical forces in order to define the reality of society, which, because of its duplicity, must appear to the uninitiated to be unreal. The problem remains, though: how are these historical forces to be appropriated, since the writer must first draw from his personal experience? The vacuum of Lovett's intellect illustrates the despair of Mailer. On the one hand, Lovett acknowledges that 'social relations, economic relations, were still independent of man's will'. Should the writer then isolate himself from society? Perhaps, but his writing talent will then atrophy: 'I lived, and was it I alone, in relation to nothing? The world would revolve, and I who might exercise a will for so long as money lasted, exercised nothing and dreamed away hours on my bed'.(117) McLeod, the Marxist, mocks Lovett's fatalistic desire to be allowed his corner in which to write, even if that talent continues. Of what value would such a book be? ' "Distinguish, man, between your own desires and the realm of political possibility" '(86) because ' "your own problems are not the problems of the world, and one's state of mind may well determine one's political outlook" '.(90)

If Lovett takes note of McLeod's advice, he is relearning lessons absorbed in his mysterious past, but they are ideas that are not his own. The only alternative left to the writer is to abandon his fictional ambitions and translate his sentiments into action. Before Lovett is fully converted to McLeod's revolutionary convictions, he reflects upon the hopelessness of action: because society operates independently of man's will, it controls his actions. It forces a soldier to kill, despite that soldier's repugnance to his military duty. Lovett concludes: 'His ideas move in one direction, and the sad feet which belong to society move in the other. Thus the actions of people and not their sentiments make history'.(117) His espousal of McLeod's cause is effected by means of realising the possibility of those 'sad feet' belonging to individuals and not society. The actions of the people may then be creative instead of created. So the novel draws to its conclusion, as Lovett pawns his typewriter, shelves his manuscript, and, armed with McLeod's legacy, the little object, studies with a view to the imaginary future when theory may be converted to effective action.

The quandary of Mickey Lovett which, in the light of Mailer's prefatory Advertisement to the reprinted extract from his novel, clearly reflects his own literary dilemma, is discussed in another context by John W. Aldridge. Aldridge feels that there is a critical resurgence of 'the idea that fiction should be read with some primary regard for the social and political views of the author'.[5] But the danger, he goes on, is that this idea may be 'antithetical to the aesthetic approach' rather than 'a further liberalization of it'.[6] From the point of view of the writer, the ability to combine individual and collective experience in a satisfactory fictional form must first overcome a serious obstacle, which is that 'we have ceased in recent years to believe in the reality and authority, the concrete *factualness*, of individual experience . . .'[7] which ultimately depends upon 'some perception of underlying social coherence, the possibility of discovering the defining metaphor of our condition'.[8] This is the problem that Mailer, with his own views upon the relationship between individual and collective experience, faces. In the absence, as yet, of the defining metaphor to which Aldridge refers, Mailer relies, as in his previous novel, upon a central symbol, which is a little object that McLeod has stolen from the government.

McLeod's admission of this theft to Hollingsworth allows him to define the sickness of society. Whether the state is communist or capitalist, it must maintain a certain level of productivity in order that the worker might have an adequate reward for his labour. To maintain an adequate standard of living, other countries' wealth must be appropriated and the economy is converted to the stockpiling of armaments. This is a self-perpetuating process. McLeod is echoing Lovett's earlier conviction that the phenomena of the world today are 'war, and the preparations for new war', (116) although the former goes on to state 'it is a war which ends as a conflict between two virtually identical forms of exploitation'.(199) The horrifying vision of the future that McLeod holds is the needs of armament taking priority over the needs of the consumer, the growth of discontent and the police state, until finally 'the intent of society will be to produce wholly for death, and men will be kept alive merely to further that aim'.(200) With war, famine and death as the only realities, mankind rushes toward barbarism.

McLeod deliberately isolates himself from the powers which he sees as being equally corrupt: the American government whom he has betrayed by his theft and the communist government to whom he would refuse to sell it. Instead, he has found solitary comfort in theory, in the writing of articles proclaiming his hope in the socialist revolution. McLeod concludes the speech in his defence by expressing a tentative faith in human potential which will oppose the state, free him of his hostile environment and enable him ' "to discover his real dilemmas and real fulfillment if there is any" '.(205) This is a deeply felt conviction held by Mailer who concludes his review of David Riesman's book *Individualism Reconsidered* in *Advertisements for Myself* by stating the aims of a socialist world: 'we feel the moral imperative in life itself to raise the human condition even if this should ultimately mean no more than that man's suffering has been lifted to a higher level, and human history has only progressed from melodrama, farce, and monstrosity, to tragedy itself'.(185) Because Mailer is unable to define any practical solution to effecting a socialist revolution, beyond McLeod's general injunction '"It is the need to study, it is the obligation to influence those few we may . . ."'(204) the novel ends on a note of deep pessimism. Lovett wanders along an endless succession of alleys, studying but helplessly watching mankind drifting ever closer to the shore of barbarism.

The presence of the little object, however, suggests that there is an alternative to the Marxist definition of consciousness. In an earlier interrogation by Hollingsworth, McLeod counters his interrogator's demands as to where and what it is by asking '"What if there is no point and only a context?"'(138) The essence of his argument is that the object's significance lies in its power to define the people, the powers that pursue it. It can control its context—it tinges Hollingsworth's departure with defeat, it triumphs over his employers, it hastens McLeod's end by pushing him to suicide, it endows Lovett with a future. It provides the means by which a man's sentiments may be converted into actions in order to discover his own dilemmas and in order to demonstrate those of society. The theft of the object from a governmental body by an individual converts the concept of revolution from the collective consciousness, as defined by Marx, to the individual consciousness. McLeod describes it as '"an end product, delivered into the world trailing corruption and gore, laden with guilt, a petrifaction of all which preceded it"'.(138–9) Its possession by McLeod and then Lovett suggests its conversion into a moral honesty. Beyond that Mailer cannot go with his redemptive symbol. Just as he could not clearly define what force Mount Anaka released in Sergeant Croft, Mailer cannot specify what change the little object effects in the individual consciousness with regard to propelling that consciousness into action.

What Mailer does effectively demonstrate, however, is the effect that the little object has upon his characters, when it is interpreted as a tangible object without regard to the context which defines it as being potentially redemptive. Hollingsworth, McLeod, Lannie and Guinevere all represent social forces which have no connection with their personal identities. The result is that they are all largely incomprehensible to Lovett, who is trapped with them for the most part in a Brooklyn boarding house. Mailer, who is forced within the confines of conventional fiction, employs the bewilderment of

Lovett and the oddities of the boarding house inmates in order to write an allegory upon the failure of the revolutionary socialist to prevent a world from sinking into a condition of barbarism.

Hollingsworth seems to be a naive, boring provincial until he is revealed as an FBI agent on the track of McLeod and his little object. Lannie's poverty and madness conceals her singleminded hatred of Trotsky's assassins, with whom she suspects McLeod was involved, which leads her to become Hollingsworth's accomplice. McLeod's timidity and loneliness is a façade behind which lies a political erudition and active involvement and his unsuccessful marriage to Guinevere. Guinevere herself is a blowsy apolitical opportunist with a precocious, larger-than-life daughter, Monina.

The first two-thirds of the novel are principally concerned with the exposure of these lies and deceptions, only to reveal that once true identities and relationships are established, the five individuals are each isolated within their own obsessions, unable to allow any real contact with each other. They persist in maintaining their deceptive roles, even after their antagonisms have been exposed. Hollingsworth disconcertingly slips from the unassuming, inexperienced manner of the provincial to a brutal seducer and canny interrogator. Guinevere effects the transition from a genteel hostess to a bawdy fishwife in the course of a single sentence. McLeod has a bewildering variety of manners, from the cynical womaniser to the timid intellectual to the intense man of conviction, not to mention his possible identity as the Balkan agent who expediently murdered two friends. The several emotions expressed by each of these characters in their many roles are false because none of them appears to exercise any control over the kind of performance they present at any time. They are patently not in control of the context in which they act, because they are not aware of it as a relevant force. As a result, they exist in the uniform tawdriness of the boarding house.

The legacy of McLeod to Lovett does, however, raise an unanswered question. How is the writer to convert his sentiments into actions and still call himself a writer? In attempting to answer this question, Mailer came close to rejecting the effectiveness of the writer's efforts, even while he still clearly valued his own literary ambitions. In his review of Riesman's book (*Advertisements for Myself*), he argued:

As serious artistic expression is the answer to the meaning of life for a few, so the passion for socialism is the only meaning I can conceive in the lives of those who are not artists; if one cannot create 'works' one may dream at least of an era when humans create humans, and the satisfaction of the radical can come from the thought that he tries to keep this idea alive.(184)

Mailer himself persisted in the conviction that if the conversion of men's sentiments into actions make history, then it must be effected through the revolution of the writer, rather than through the revolution of the politicised intellectual.

The interpretation of history is a crucial one for Mailer at this stage in his career. He uses it in 'The Man Who Studied Yoga' (1952), in his review of Riesman's book, in his third novel *The Deer Park* and, concluding *Advertisements for Myself* he repeats it, observing 'the best sentence I've ever written—but I would hate to face eternity with that for my flag, since I am still at this formal middle of my life a creator of sentiments larger than my work'.(391) This is acute self-criticism. The hostile environment in 'The Man Who Studied Yoga' and the review is more closely defined than Lovett's abstract criticisms of social and economic relations. It is, in the story, the dishonesty of the press and in the review, the mass-communications media. Both forces oppress the individual with words that are empty of meaning; words that, as John W. Aldridge argues 'are becoming more and more our substitutes for experience'.[9] It is the *writer's* responsibility, according to Mailer, to counteract these false words and the synthetic experience they embody, with true ones that create a historical reality through the presentation of an immediate means of action.

In 'The Man Who Studied Yoga', the legacy that McLeod passed on to Lovett of study, work and faith in a socialist revolution is stripped, in the sodden realism of this story, to a futile gesture. Sam Slovoda knows he is a fool to suffer for idealistic radical principles, but cannot resist relishing the self-pitying bond with his old friend Marvin Rossman with whom he was a member of the communist party in the 1930s. But if Sam's political principles have failed him, so has his ambition to write a novel. It remains a formless mass of notes and ideas without a hero.

The root cause of Sam's creative impotence lies in the fact that he has placed his intellect in a vacuum. 'He rejects the world with his intellect, and this enables him not to face the more direct realities of his present life'.(151) Sam indulges in a pornographic fantasy by copulating with his wife in front of an erotic film in order that he may abnegate responsibility for his unhappiness. He dreams of the past and deceives himself about the future in order to escape from the present. The story takes its title from a story told by Sam's friend Alan Sperber. The dilemma of Cassius O'Shaugnessy illustrates the comic absurdity of Sam's predicament. After three years of contemplation, Cassius accepts his reward and begins to unscrew his navel: ' "At the edge of revelation, I took one sweet breath, and turned my navel free . . . Damn," said Cassius, "if my ass didn't fall off".'(160)

Mailer explains in *Advertisements for Myself* that he intended this story to be the prologue to an eight-part novel, of which *The Deer Park* was to be the first. This 'descendant of *Moby Dick*'(143) died of obscurity after the first draft of *The Deer Park* was completed, but 'The Man Who Studied Yoga' was conceived and written with this grand and complex scheme in mind. The result is that the story is narrated by a faceless and omniscient observer whom Mailer was wise not to omit, in order to make the story 'more neatly complete in itself'.(144) The omniscience of the point of view releases the story from the circumscribed bleakness of Sam Slovoda's life into a tantalising if grim glimpse of the direct realities of American society at present. The stifling impasse of the corrupt media can be countered not by a dead familiarity with economic terms, such as Sam has inherited from the Depression years, but with madness or religion—the unexplored and metaphysical regions of the con-sciousness. The story concludes with a message from the narrator to Sam who lies in bed haunted by the failure of his ambition to write a novel. 'In the middle from wakefulness to slumber, in the torpor which floats beneath the blankets, I give an idea to Sam. "Destroy time, and chaos may be ordered," I say to him.'(171) The meaning of this final injunction is ambiguous in the context of Mailer's story, other than being a general warning to ignore everything that lacks the immediacy of self-creation and to maintain the courage to defend that self-creation.

The story is, as Mailer himself immediately recognised, a qualified achievement. It helped him through the realisation that *The Deer Park*, as the first draft stood, would 'die of obscurity and a tortured style unless I gave way to a simpler novel which was coming forward from my characters'.(143) But the fictional expression of effective individual revolution was still divorced from its means of embodiment in the world. Mount Anaka and the little object remain unsatisfactory symbols in *The Naked and the Dead* and *Barbary Shore* and although the implications of the narrator's injunction to Sam in 'The Man Who Studied Yoga' is a theme that is developed in *The Deer Park*, it fails to solve a similar problem in Mailer's third novel.

Although Mailer says he abandoned the idea of *The Deer Park* as the first part of an eight-part novel, the project is again introduced, though in an equivocal tone, in the final Advertisement to 'The Time of Her Time' and 'Advertisements For Myself On The Way Out'. The latter is now to be the Prologue, 'The Time of Her Time' will appear fifty or a hundred pages later. The idea of this eight-part novel gave *The Deer Park* an importance in Mailer's imagination that was disproportionate to the actual achievement. But when the first draft of *The Deer Park* was rejected by Stanley Rinehart, the publisher, on the grounds of a scene of fellatio which Mailer refused to omit, his novel suddenly confirmed the contempt and distrust for society that he had previously expressed in *The Naked and the Dead* and *Barbary Shore*. It also exacerbated his increasing loss of faith in the conventional novel, and, what was most crucial to Mailer, the status of the novelist.

The lengthy Advertisement, which describes the extensive revision of the first draft of *The Deer Park*, establishments Mailer's laudable but misconceived ambitions. Charley Eitel, a talented film director, like Captain Hilliard and Lieutenant Hearn, possesses a rigid sense of integrity. He is blacklisted from the film industry because of his alleged association with communist party members, but refuses to testify before a Congressional Investigating Committee. But Eitel's integrity can only remain intact if he maintains a clear distinction between himself and the corrupt world which surrounds him. The artist, he believes, 'was always divided between his desire for power in the world and his desire for power over his work'.[10] Eitel chooses the latter but in doing so finds that he has unwittingly compromised not only his principles but his talent. He realises, too late, that in making this false distinction, he has ignored 'that law of life so cruel and so just which demanded that one must grow or else pay more for remaining the same'.(322) Mailer intends that his narrator, Sergius O'Shaugnessy, should learn the truth of this law and put it into practice. But, as in the case of Sergeant Croft and Mickey Lovett, Mailer cannot find a satisfactory means of dramatising O'Shaugnessy's ambition in his novel.

Mailer's principal problem was the narrative voice of O'Shaugnessy. The Advertisement to the novel in *Advertisements for Myself* confirms that Mailer had begun unwittingly to use his fiction as a vehicle to project his own ambitions.

> The first person seemed to paralyse me, as if I had a horror of creating a voice which could be in any way bigger than myself. So I had become mired in a false style for every narrator I tried . . . But the punishment was commencing for me. I was now creating a man who was braver and stronger than me, and the more any new style succeeded, the more I was writing an implicit portrait of myself as well.(203–4)

O'Shaugnessy is shaped by Mailer's ideas on what *should* constitute a process of self-creation, not by the progress of a plot which suggests that this is a process *chosen* by the protagonist. O'Shaugnessy, therefore, effects a moral growth that is independent of the world in which he moves. While we are intended to believe that his choice to grow more has its source in the exercise of his will, it appears to be the deterministic imposition of force of circumstance. As a flier in the Air Force, O'Shaugnessy had always regarded killing and the possibility of being killed impersonally. Yet being in close quarters with a Japanese boy whose arm has been badly burned forces O'Shaugnessy to regard the act of dropping jellied gasolene bombs from the victim's point of view. In Desert D'Or, he concludes

> I had the idea there were two worlds. There was a real world as I called it, a world of wars and boxing clubs and children's homes on back streets, and this real world was a world where orphans burned orphans. It was better not even to think of this. I liked the other world in which almost everybody lived. The imaginary world.(51)

At this point, O'Shaugnessy's literary ambition is based upon a false distinction. For his imagination will, in fact, atrophy, if he ignores the real world which is that part of himself that he has chosen to ignore for its unpleasant connotations. But the false and hypocritical world of Desert D'Or provides O'Shaugnessy with a necessary experience that can convince him of the necessity of the real world to his talent. The world of Collie Munshin, Herman Teppis and Supreme Pix is an imaginary world in the sense that it provides an escape for O'Shaugnessy. But when he realises that he is motivated by cowardice and self-delusion, this world provides an important criterion by which the real world may be judged and valued with renewed vigour.

The occasion on which this about-face is effected is when O'Shaugnessy refuses to sign the contract that Collie Munshin offers him, which would ensure him a successful film career.

> The closer I came to wanting the contract, the more he bothered me, and all the while Collie would go on or Lulu would go on, painting my career with words, talking about the marvellous world, the real world, about all the good things which would happen to me, and all the while I was thinking they were wrong, and the real world was underground—a tangle of wild caves where orphans burned orphans.(209)

Suddenly the nature of Desert D'Or's hypocrisy is revealed; it illustrates the duplicity of words when they are divorced from the reality of their meaning. If the real world, where words and their reality are conjoined, is abruptly located in an underground tangle of caves, it is because Mailer is attempting to locate this real world within O'Shaugnessy. Since orphans represent his disturbing past, the underground tangle of caves is an image of his unconscious which must be resuscitated before he can be a successful artist. After his momentous decision, he cannot make love to his beautiful mistress, Lulu Meyers, without thinking of 'bursting flesh, rotting flesh, flesh hung on spikes in butcher stalls, flesh burning, flesh gone to blood'.(214) The images confirm the irrevocable nature of his decision.

Yet this real world, by which we are to measure the decadent chains of the Hollywood world, is no more than melodramatic rhetoric in the mouth of O'Shaugnessy. It describes Mailer's disgust with the Eisenhower years and the Korean War rather than a harsh reality which forces O'Shaugnessy's painful but courageous exit from Hollywood. Similarly, the exercise of O'Shaugnessy's imagination as he tells his story does not describe the difficulties of the narrator: it demonstrates the difficulties of the author. When

O'Shaugnessy must describe events that he has not witnessed, which principally concern the fates of Charley Eitel and his mistress, Elena Esposito, he must become a novelist who is 'A galley-slave to his imagination so he can look for the truth'.(96)

In order for Mailer to dramatise the false distinction between the real and imaginary world, he introduces Marion Faye, the son of a gossip columnist and a pimp by profession. In O'Shaugnessy, the conjunction of an individual's creativity and the world which surrounds it is incomplete, because the life he adopts when he moves on from Desert D'Or is indeterminately focused upon grand literary ambitions. These are founded upon the conviction that no other writer 'could begin to be a final authority for me, because finally the crystallization of their experience did not have a texture apposite to my experience, and I had the conceit, I had the intolerable conviction, that I would write about worlds I knew better than anyone alive'.(330) Faye, on the other hand, converts O'Shaugnessy's melodramatic expression of the reconstituted self in the real world into practical experience.

In conversation with Sergius, he remarks ' "There is no pleasure greater than that obtained from a conquered repugnance" '(139) to which Sergius rejoins by substituting the word vice for repugnance. Faye responds ' "Nobility and vice—they're the same thing. It just depends on the direction you're going" '.(140) Faye is countering Sergius' social morality with a personal one, which puts into focus the meaning of O'Shaugnessy's breakdown while in the Air Force. To kill *en masse* and be indifferent through ignorance is immoral; it is the realisation of this immorality that breaks O'Shaugnessy when he sees the Japanese boy's burned arm. But when Faye faces the impulse to kill within himself, he insists, through his suffering, that this is not immoral, but the courageous subversion of a world that O'Shaugnessy theoretically despises. In pursuing that cruel but just law of life, which is that one must grow according to a personal morality that will regard vice and nobility as interchangeable qualities, Mailer is an example, Diana Trilling argues, of 'the modern imagination [which] apparently takes the heroic leap only at some cost in moral logic'.[11]

Although the form of Mailer's essay 'The White Negro' justifies this objection, the philosophy of Marion Faye, which is a precursor to that essay, does not. Faye, the only person to effect a dramatically convincing revolt against Desert D'Or's hell of manufactured sex, pays the price of intense suffering in conquering his repugnance. He lies in a constant sweat of terror at night because he forces himself not to lock his door. In callously refusing a fix to Paco, a pathetic Mexican, he burns at the compassion he has refused in himself because 'Compassion was the queen to guilt'.(151) When he finally faces the command within himself to kill Elena, by encouraging her suicide, he is not a 'victim at the mercy of his own psycho-pathology'.[12] Faye is acknowledging a fact that O'Shaugnessy did not have the courage to face. All men possess the impulse to kill; it is more courageous to accept the responsibility for a personal act than to accept an impersonal endorsement to kill millions as Sergius had done from his aeroplane. Honesty is the key word in Faye's philosophy: honesty to admit the nature of social corruption, which is that sentiment masquerades as love and vice as nobility. As Faye suggests, when he equates nobility with vice, he exposes both the evil and goodness of life by assuming the qualities of either according to the exigencies of a particular situation. This endows Faye with the heretical vision 'that God was the Devil and the One they called the Devil was God-in-banishment like a noble prince deprived of true Heaven, and God who was the Devil had conquered except for the few who saw the cheat that God was not God at all'.(308) Faye converts his subversive philosophy into a metaphysical drama that, in this context, only obliquely suggests the subsequent development of Mailer's metaphorical oppositions. Murder, as yet, is a literal and realistic possibility in this novel, which Faye ultimately withdraws from. After refusing Paco his heroin fix, Faye drives out into the desert, in order to see the dawn. The sunrise is associated in his mind with a nuclear holocaust for which he passionately prays: 'Let it come, Faye begged, like a man praying for rain, let it come and clear the rot and the stench and the stink, let it come for all of everywhere, just so it comes and the world stands clear in the white dead dawn'.(152) The destruction of the world will save Faye from the suffering caused by his individual exposure of the world's rot, stench and stink. His terror at realising that 'he must coax Elena to kill herself'(308) is superseded by his complete despair after the relief at finding he has failed. 'Faye knew he was defeated. He could not help it—he had his drop of mercy after all'.(317) This mercy forces Mailer to cast Faye in the role of a martyr, destroyed by a society whose sickness he effectively mirrored. Although the nature of his demise is less justified, he is defeated, like Croft and Cummings, by the trivial operation of chance. While taking Elena to the airport he crashes his car, which results in a conviction for possessing a gun without a licence.

In his honest confrontation with the murderous impulse within himself, Faye clearly prefigures Mailer's existential hipster. But the sexual theme in *The Deer Park* also prepared Mailer for his development of sexual metaphors in 'The White Negro'. In *The Naked and the Dead* and *Barbary Shore*, the sexuality of the characters illustrates the extent to which external social forces manipulate and oppress the individual. In *The Deer Park*, it is also potentially redemptive. Although it is quite probable that Mailer began *The Deer Park* with the intention of concentrating his theme upon the political corruption of the early 1950s, the compromise that Eitel eventually makes to the Congressional Investigating Committee is caused by the failure of his affair with Elena Esposito.

If Mailer was beginning to feel pessimistic about the possibilities of a political revolution, the setting of Hollywood with its outspoken but insincere sexuality must have suggested an interesting and relevant counterpoint to the struggle of Eitel and Elena to create a relationship founded upon the tenderness of genuine love. It is always a counterpoint: Eitel and Elena's love stands or falls on their own willpower to maintain it *despite* the influence of the society that surrounds them. Although they fail because, as Mailer argues, in *Advertisements for Myself*, 'they are finally not brave enough, and so do more damage to one another than to the unjust world outside them'(204), the possibility for personal growth that Eitel glimpses in the course of the affair becomes a legacy that he passes on to Sergius.

Both Eitel and Elena are people of enormous sexual talent and experience; they know how to please one another with their inventive techniques. But according to the laws of sex 'borrow technique in place of desire, and sexlike life would demand the debt be paid . . .'.(191) Eitel ceases to desire Elena, even though their technique remains as resourceful as ever, because he cannot overcome his snobbery which insists on making him see Elena as common, coarse, even whorish. Elena ceases to desire Eitel because she cannot overcome her inability to love and her conviction that sex is a commodity. Ultimately, neither is able to feel aroused unless desire is 'as exciting as the pages of a pornographic text where one could read in safety and not grudge every emotion the woman felt for another man'.(192) It is the fear of risking giving oneself to another and the safety of putting, like the rest of Desert D'Or, an economic value on sex, that is the mark of Eitel's downfall, just as it is the symptom of Sam Slovoda's emotional and creative sterility in 'The Man Who Studied Yoga'. Appropriately enough, Eitel uses a sexual metaphor to describe his capitulation to the Investigating Committee: ' "So for the first time in my life I had the sensation of being a complete and total whore in the world . . ." '.(283) Unlike Eitel, Faye uses sex like a weapon. He defiantly refuses to attach any value to it other than an economic one, in order to prove his independence from and superiority to the society that treats sex in no other way but which pretends otherwise. He is subverting a man like Herman Teppis, who will scream that homosexuality is a disease, pour asinine platitudes on the nature of love, framing it all in the context of box-office sales, and then immediately pay for a call girl to perform fellatio upon him.

The sexual theme illustrates the genesis of Mailer's revolution, for which he still had to find a suitable form. The failure of *The Deer Park* left Mailer determined to employ any means that would break down the barrier between the truths expressed in his writing and the truths that are felt because they are lived out. In his review of *Waiting for Godot* Mailer uses Beckett's play to clarify his despair with regard to his own impotence as a writer. 'Beckett's work brings our despair to the surface, it nourishes it with air, and therefore alters it . . .'.(262) The realisation leads Mailer to define the artist's purpose, which is to create a human consciousness that 'can express itself in action and so alter society'.(ibid) He makes no distinction here between the artist and his creation, so that when he introduces 'the creative nihilism of the Hip', (ibid) it is not clear whether 'the Hip' exists imaginatively or literally. Nevertheless, Mailer's purpose is clear, as he defines 'the Hip' as an agent of violent change which is redemptive because 'the violence is better without than within, better as individual actions than as the collective murders of society . . .'.(ibid)

Mailer had therefore all but created a social, rather than purely imaginative type who is a violent agent of change, whose actions are dictated by his senses rather than by his intellect. But the relationship between the hipster and the artist remains unclear. Another essay in *Advertisements for Myself* called 'From Surplus Value to The Mass-Media' suggests that the 'new revolutionary vision of society' seems to exist independently of the artist. If he can capture this vision in his work, then 'it will explore not nearly so far into that jungle of political economy which Marx charted and so opened to rapid development, but rather will engage the empty words, dead themes, and sentimental voids of that mass-media whose internal contradictions twist and quarter us between the lust of the economy . . .',(356) but this ability is not ensured.

As a result, the form of 'The White Negro' demonstrates both Mailer's fear 'that I was no longer a writer',(269) and his determination to revolutionise literary form in order to allay that fear. His existential hipster is the kind of ideal or representative type that had already been used in the work of sociologists during this period, such as David Riesman in his book *The Lonely Crowd*. But in the context of 'The White Negro', the hipster also assumes the proportions of a fictional protagonist, even while Mailer has carefully abandoned fictional boundaries. It is as if the plot of *Barbary Shore* had reached its climax with the revelation that Lovett had invented the characters in the boarding house. Yet Lovett is a character; Mailer in this sense is not. The boundary of aesthetic form does not exist; the fiction hipster, with his frightening programme of action, moves quite literally into the streets. He is murderous and exhibits moral indifference to the consequences of his actions. Nevertheless, Mailer insists that with the removal of 'every social restraint or category man would become more creative than murderous and so would not destroy himself'.(286) The process by which Mailer defines this creativity is built upon the observation: 'if society was so murderous' through the legitimised horror of warfare, then it is courageously honest to face 'the most hideous of questions about [the individual's] own nature . . .',(271) because this crippled and perverted society is man's collective creation. The transformation of this collective creation into an individual one is potentially redemptive because it can establish a causality, and therefore a purpose to life that will substitute 'the Faustian urge' of civilisation, which is

> to dominate nature by mastering time, mastering the links of social cause and effect—in the middle of an economic civilization founded upon the confidence that time could indeed be subjected to our will, our psyche was subjected itself to the intolerable anxiety that death being causeless, life was causeless as well, and time deprived of cause and effect had come to a stop.(270)

In action, the hipster is literally a psychopathic murderer. But Mailer employs a series of images to suggest the creativity that is inherent in this conventionally immoral activity. The hipster possesses 'a new nervous system',(277) he employs the therapy of a good orgasm, he expresses the buried infant within himself and represents 'the affirmation of the barbarian, for it requires a primitive passion about human nature to believe that individual acts of violence are always to be preferred to the collective violence of the State . . .'.(286) Yet Mailer does not conceive of Hip as being a complete escape into a primitive, instinctive mode of being. He told Richard Stern 'we're all civilized, and to return to the senses and keep the best parts of our civilized being, to keep our capacity for mental organization, for mental construction, for logic is doubly difficult . . .'.(311) This conception of man, precariously balancing the civilised and primitive aspects of his nature and striving to capitalise on the advantages of both, stresses that aspect of Mailer's writing which links him with the American nineteenth-century imagination. In his preface to the collected edition of *The Leatherstocking Tales*, James Fenimore Cooper wrote of Natty Bumppo: 'removed from nearly all the temptations of civilized life, placed in the best associations of that which is deemed savage, and favourably disposed by nature to improve such advantages, it appeared to the writer that his hero was a fit subject to represent the better qualities of both conditions, without pushing either to extremes'.[13] Cooper places his hero in a historically recognisable wilderness, while Mailer's wilderness is a state of consciousness that manifests itself in a series of socially irresponsible acts. Nevertheless, the existential hipster belongs to that nineteenth-century tradition of the American hero begun by Cooper, Thoreau and Whitman. As Leslie Fiedler has pointed out: 'One does not become a child of nature in the nineteenth century by attempting to eschew culture; one becomes, in so far as he fails, a *literary* version of the child of nature; and in so far as he succeeds, a creature of subculture . . .'.[14]

Yet the fact remains that although Mailer has clearly defined the nature of his revolutionary group, his confusing and ambiguous use of literal and figurative terms of reference makes it impossible to conceive of how the hipster will change society. The essay characterises this type as acting individually and impulsively, which contradicts the implicit assumption that the hipster, prompted by the Negro, will emerge as a coherent revolutionary group. As a result, society hardly seems necessary to the hipster's rebellion.

Mailer attempted to solve this logical contradiction by arguing that the intersection of the hipster and his social context at the moment of self-definition be given a linguistic creativity. Yet Mailer cannot resort to a formal aesthetic, neither can he speak with any authority as a writer since he has deliberately undermined the traditional security of that position. Instead, he discusses the hipster's language whose words gain meaning when 'the nuance of the voice uses the nuance of the situation to convey the subtle contextual difference'.(281) It cannot be taught; if the language is not used in conjunction with the experience it describes, 'then it seems merely arch or vulgar or irritating'.(280)

Robert Lucid and Richard Stern illustrate the confusion of Mailer's relationship to his hipster in the course of the interview conducted by Stern. Mailer establishes that the hipster gambles with death and the novelist gambles with his talent. Lucid objects to the presumption of an analogous sense of purpose on the part of the hipster and novelist because ' "the whole notion of Hip is, in fact, unconscious, it is mere action" '.(314) Stern qualifies Lucid's remark by distinguishing between the hipster's ' "personal being" ' and the novelist's ' "talent as a novelist" '.(ibid) Lucid disallows this by insisting that the novelist is conscious of the moral consequences of his decision while the hipster must be ' "unconscious of risks of this kind, of the profundity . . ." '.(ibid) Mailer concludes by emphasising that the unconscious has the power to provide the hipster with a subliminal sense of purpose at the moment of each existential act: '"the unconscious, you see, has an enormous teleological sense . . . it moves towards a goal . . . it has real sense of what is happening to one's being at each given moment . . . It is with this thing that they move, that they grope forward—this navigator at the seat of their being"'. (ibid) Mailer applies this idea of the navigator of the unconscious to his own creative process nine years later[15] and in a context that brings the interesting implications of the theory to fruition. But his rejoinder to Lucid and Stern's remarks does not resolve the lack of a controlling fictionalist who can create and control the relationship between the hipster's actions and the language that describes those actions.

Although the nature of the hipster's rebellion is uncertainly figurative in 'The White Negro', Mailer successfully dramatises the creative implications of this rebellion in 'The Time of Her Time', which is his finest short story. The description of the hipster's search for a good orgasm suggests that he may recreate his selfhood through his sexual activity. But this activity appears to be literally argued and therefore represents the return of the whole self to the senses, which, from the point of view of the hipster, is an achieved thing.

The sexual activity of Sergius O'Shaugnessy in 'The Time of Her Time' is a metaphor for Mailer's creative will and therefore represents only that part of himself which is concerned with the process of creation.

O'Shaugnessy is the narrator and protagonist and has an outrageous attitude toward sex:

> I was cold, maybe by birth, certainly by environment . . . I was going now on a kind of disinterested but developed competence . . . I had my good looks, my blond hair, my height, build, and bullfighting school, I suppose I became one of the village equivalents to an Eagle Scout badge for the girls. I was one of the credits needed for a diploma in the sexual humanities.(398)

O'Shaugnessy is a dramatised version of the existential hipster. He exists on the edge of society; his room is at the top of a Greenwich Village tenement building, his women are only on loan from 'boyfriend, lover, mate or husband . . .'.(398) He fits precisely Mailer's definition of Hip, which is 'the sophistication of the wise primitive in a giant jungle . . .'.(275) He is surrounded by the barbarians of southern Manhattan and teaches the art of bullfighting in his attic apartment.

The tone of O'Shaugnessy's voice is consistently detached; his eye for detail is clinical and cold. While he is Hip and therefore a member of an 'élite', O'Shaugnessy's story, which is the description of his three sexual encounters with Denise Gondelman, emphasises the inconsistency of the tone in which it is told. He develops a growing admiration for Denise since she is unusual in that she proves to be his sexual equal. Denise has the same kind of potential ruthlessness as O'Shaugnessy—arrogance with a streak of viciousness—and she also possesses courage. In bed together for the first time, O'Shaugnessy uses the image of the boxing match to emphasise her independence and her response to the rules of the fighting exchange. A blow across the face brings her near to an orgasm. Yet Denise fails to achieve a climax because, in the terminology of the story's title, her time is still social time, her mentality and therefore her actions are rigidly controlled by the hopeless contradictions of society. O'Shaugnessy's description of her slipping away from her orgasm reflects this rigidity: 'she made a mistake, her will *ordered* all temptings and rhythms to *mobilize* their *march*, she drove into hard stupidities of a *marching-band's* step . . .'.(403, my italics) What Denise cannot do is learn from her situation, which is the prerequisite of self-creation. In 'The White Negro', Mailer emphasises the importance of context in the philosophy of Hip.

> Hip sees the context as generally dominating the man, dominating him because his character is less significant than the context in which he must function. Since it is arbitrarily five times more demanding of one's energy to accomplish even an inconsequential action in an unfavourable context than a favourable one, man is then not only his character but his context, since the success or failure of an action in a given context reacts upon the character and therefore affects what the character will be in the next context. What dominates both character and context is the energy available at the moment of intense context.(285)

It is in her use of language that Denise demonstrates her shortcoming. When O'Shaugnessy first meets her, she discusses the poetry of T. S. Eliot in the mannered pretentious terminology of fashionable academics. They then go on to talk about her analyst, Stanford Joyce, whom she admires as much as Eliot. Her language is peppered with psychoanalytical terms she has picked up from Joyce; she escapes behind terminology to defend herself from her failure to achieve an orgasm with Arthur, her boyfriend. Mailer scorns psychoanalysis in 'The White Negro' as a 'psychic bloodletting'.(278) It does not alter the patient so much as wear him out—a fate to which Denise is prone.

Since his second encounter is even emptier than the first, O'Shaugnessy determines in the third and final one to immortalise himself in her memory, to conquer her indifference, by giving her her first orgasm. He lives according to personal Time and so is qualified to convert Denise's time into her Time, to force her to abandon social cupidities and to submit to Sergius, both physically and mentally. In the marathon session which finally brings her to submit and experience an orgasm, O'Shaugnessy operates coldly and with calculation. His lovemaking has all the qualities of a well-planned campaign in which he works on her 'like a riveter, knowing her resistances were made of steel . . .'.(413) He abandons her, waits till she unwillingly pleads for more and then buggers her. When he feels her hanging back, he says ' "You dirty little Jew" '(414) which finally carries her to her climax. Although she departs with hatred in her eyes for what he has done, she is irrevocably conquered. She will never be the same again, not only because she has achieved the time of her Time, but because O'Shaugnessy has achieved the time of his Time by making himself immortal in her memory.

The pace of the story never loses its dynamism, and often the arresting imagery combines humour with economic precision: 'I lay low, eyes all closed, under sexual water, like a submarine listening for the distant sound of her ship's motors, hoping to steal up close and trick her rhythms away'.(413–14) Yet this kind of prose style reinforces the detachment in O'Shaugnessy's voice; it remains cool and measured even as he is describing the most frenetic of sexual adventures. It needs to be, of course, since he is interested in recording action and its implications in the allusive language he uses to describe it. In the decisive lovemaking session, for example, Denise is abandoned in her 'baffled heat' and then buggered by O'Shaugnessy's 'avenger'.(414) He describes his sensory awareness of her body in a proliferation of natural imagery: the mounting of waves which leave O'Shaugnessy 'hardly moving for fear of damping this quake from her earth . . .'.(ibid) Her vagina smells of the sea which indicates to O'Shaugnessy that she is near a climax. O'Shaugnessy is literally creating a new experience for Denise, but he is also creating, in an artistic sense, since he is releasing language from sterile, rigid concepts into the immediacy of a specific situation. Denise's use (or abuse) of language is the counterpoint to O'Shaugnessy's.

His determination to be immortalised in her memory therefore takes on an added layer of meaning. As he lies exhausted after giving Denise her orgasm, he whispers to himself ' "Compliments of T. S. Eliot" ',(415) and submerged beneath the obvious irony is the implication that this is the way to understand the nature of artistic creation, not by forcing it into critical terminology formulated in a mental vacuum. To be immortalised in Denise's memory, therefore, is to have one's creative act immortalised through one's individual language, no matter how much reluctant hatred might accompany the recognition of such an achievement. In 'The Time of Her Time', Mailer can dramatise the connection between an individual act and the language that is used to describe that act, because O'Shaugnessy is both the narrator and the protagonist. Mailer can express 'abstract states of feeling'(273) because the fictional form allows him metaphorically to express the notion of individual creativity.

Even though 'The Time of Her Time' is a remarkable achieve-ment, the conventional form of fiction still sealed Mailer's re-volutionary intentions from political, social and cultural forces. The form of *Advertisements for Myself* however, solved this problem. The printed extracts that follow Mailer's writing career from its inception to the time that this book went to press, trace the development of his literary protagonists. In this respect, Mailer, as the self-appointed 'General' of his columns in *The Village Voice*, is the same kind of fictional invention as the existential hipster in the reprinted 'The White Negro' or the more conventional characters of his early short stories. The activities of these protagonists with-in their own particular fictions unselfconsciously illustrate the larger purpose of the book in which they are included. *Advertise-ments for Myself* is given a purposeful form by a retrospective voice who provides an interpretive context to his fictions, called 'Ad-vertisements'. When he discovered with horror that O'Shaug-nessy in *The Deer Park* was an implicit self-portrait, Mailer felt that he was dishonestly transgressing the boundary of the novel. But Mailer's notions on the fiction of identity which had been exhaustively explored in a thematic sense, were demonstrated in the form of *Advertisements for Myself* because he could fictionalise himself. He is both a struggling writer in a literal sense (in his columns, essays, reviews and interviews) and in a metaphorical one (in his novel extracts and short stories); and a detached critic, as the author of the 'Advertisements'.

By means of creating a series of fictional identities whose activities simultaneously enact and comment upon a literary career that declares its generalised cultural commitment, Mailer had success-fully transformed rather than ignored his fictional boundaries. He also confidently mocks those readers who would assume that, since he had entered the real world by means of apparently autobiog-raphical narration, there should be, at least somewhere, a real Norman Mailer with a consistent, logical and responsible identity. In his review of *Making It* by Norman Podhoretz, which was written in 1968, Mailer illustrates the purpose of the form of *Advertisements for Myself*. After specifying that one can only term such a personal work an autobiography if it is written at the end of the writer's career, he goes on:

But when a man writes a book about himself in the beginning or middle of his career, then his work if at all penetrating is not a biography so much as a special category of fiction, precisely because his choices for future career are still open . . . So he must make that same creative abstraction from life that a novelist makes when he cooks up or conceives a character out of one or more people he partially comprehends.[16]

One of Mailer's principal objections to Podhoretz's book is that he fails to meet one of the most difficult demands of this special character of fiction: 'that one must succeed in creating a character who is not fatally separate to those who know the author and those who don't'.(184) Mailer's writing after *Advertisements for Myself* develops this premise. In his subsequent novels and works of fictional journalism, this type of character can shape a narrative, by means of an objective point of view, into a form built upon recollection. But he simultaneously possesses a subjective point of view that attempts to choose his own particular fictions within that narrative. Mailer concludes his review of Podhoretz's book by firmly precluding the assumption that this type of character is the invention of an idiosyncratic egotist. His literary manoeuvres always function as cultural determinants: 'It's the tragedy of us all that the consummate moment of affirmation, outright confession, or sheer renunciation now appears out of a mirror whose first question becomes: Is this noble act the work of a whack or the superbest put-on of all?'(197)

2 'The Existential Hero' and the 'Bitch Goddess'

In *Advertisements for Myself*, the interaction between the narrator and the several fictional protagonists ultimately betrays a garrulous and uncompromising attitude toward a world whose duplicity primarily serves to illustrate the public fate of Normal Mailer. The two collections of public writing that Mailer published in the 1960s demonstrate a marked change. The voice that links the articles is quieter, more obviously dedicated to the subject of them, while Mailer's point of view in these articles possesses, for the most part, a secure fictional control over the material. Although *The Presidential Papers* was published in 1963 and *Cannibals and Christians* five years later (a time lapse that records the progression from Mailer's cautious optimism during the Kennedy administration to his open woe during Johnson's years in office), there are important themes which are common to both collections. These books reveal an assurance in Mailer's prose style and in his stance toward his choice of subject matter which enabled him to return to the novel which he had deserted ten years earlier.

But the development of Mailer's narrators in the articles included in these two collections is not only due to his improved technique. In 1960 at the Democratic Convention in Los Angeles, John Kennedy was nominated and Mailer, who attended, felt immense excitement at the possibility the nomination offered for America if this man were elected President. Several months later, Mailer decided to announce his candidacy for the mayoralty of New York and on 19 November, three days before his planned announcement, he gave a party. In the early morning, after a disastrous evening, he stabbed his wife, Adele Morales, barely missing her heart. Mailer realised his loss was not so much the chance of becoming mayor, but the fact that ' "I lost any central purchase I had on the right to say what is happening . . . Now when I argue the times are violent, they can say, well, look what he did" '.[1] He had carried out to the letter the kind of violence advocated in 'The White Negro' and discovered ' "it was phony . . . It wasn't me" '.² The shock of the experience and the determination that his writing should not suffer must have contributed a great deal to the comparatively controlled tone of *The Presidential Papers*. It was also in 1960 that Mailer wrote his first piece of political journalism, after his attendance at the Democratic Convention. Although his appreciation of Kennedy was qualified from the first encounter and although his suspicions were confirmed when the Bay of Pigs was invaded and when America escalated her involvement in Vietnam, there were qualities in Kennedy that not only provoked Mailer to address a book to him, but which also inspired the genesis of Mailer's theories on the nature of politics. These theories led to his later development of personae that incorporate both the rebel and the society against which he is rebelling.

In Mailer's article, 'Superman Comes to the Supermarket', which opens *The Presidential Papers*, Kennedy is an enigma to the reporter as the latter contemplates the effect this man has upon the delegates at the Democratic Convention in Los Angeles and upon himself. Not only does Kennedy give the impression of being a 'great box-office actor'(51) but, what is even more disturbing, there is a part of his personality which remains mysterious because 'the role was one thing and the man another . . .'.(59) Yet despite the fact that Kennedy evades complete understanding, the reporter champions the candidate because, he argues, the variety of roles that Kennedy apparently has at his command overcomes the conventionality of his political utterances. The reporter's fascination for Kennedy lies in the fact that the candidate has apparently taken command of the conventional mind in order to win an election without diminishing his aura of charismatic individualism. What increasingly arouses Mailer's depression is that he finds it impossible to know which side of Kennedy possesses the superior strength—the conventional mind or the 'heroic' individualist. Nevertheless, in this article, the reporter extends this dichotomy that he sees in Kennedy to a survey of society and opposes 'the life of politics' and 'the life of myth . . . '.(54) The former is 'concrete, factual and unbelievably dull'(51) because it rigidly favours the programme, ideology or concept rather than the unpredictable, fluid acts of the individual which is termed, in the introduction to the article, 'the new psychological realities . . .'.(38) To suppress these acts is to encourage the growth of cancer or plague, which is

Mailer's expression for totalitarianism. This term is not employed in the conventional sense by Mailer, but denotes 'the creation of men as interchangeable as commodities, their extremes of personality singed out of existence . . .'.(52) Although the American myth of renaissance man no longer has its archetype in public men and has to turn to neo-renaissance man of the screen, the urge for freedom and adventure is no less valid for its being experienced vicariously. This urge constitutes 'the real subterranean life of America . . .'.(38)

The narrator of the article poses as a conventional reporter, but his description of the events that intuits this mythical, subterranean life is fictional. Mailer faced a major problem that he would completely overcome in *The Armies of the Night*, which is to convincingly establish a direct connection between the public participants of the event and the perceptions of his protagonist. Although the personae of *The Armies of the Night*, *Miami and the Siege of Chicago* and *St George and the Godfather* clearly achieve this connection, it is the style of the narrator in 'Superman Comes to the Supermarket' which dramatises the conventional and mythical realities that he perceives, even though it is occasionally tentatively managed.

The authority of the perceiving eye establishes the superficial reality of conventional politics, as for example in the description of the Biltmore Hotel which is the headquarters of the Democratic Convention. It is a depressing sight and suggests a uniform totalitarianism, not because the presence of the Devil and his commitment to waste is metaphorically invoked, but because the power of the prose, full of sickeningly dying colours does not describe dull nausea; it is dully nauseating.

> The Gallery of the Biltmore, that huge depressing alley with its inimitable hotel color, that faded depth of chiaroscuro which unhappily has no depth, that brown which is not a brown, that grey which has no pearl in it, that color which can be described only as hotel-color because the beiges, the tans, the walnuts, the mahoganies, the dull blood rugs, the moaning yellows, the sick greens, the greys and all those dumb browns merge into that lack of color which is an over-large hotel at convention time . . . .(47)

Similarly, the style with which the protagonist observes the public figures reconstitutes them in a manner that exposes the corruption of their exercise of power: 'Bob Wagner, the mayor of New York, a little man, plump, groomed, blank. He had the blank, pomaded, slightly worried look of the first barber in a good barbershop, the kind who would go to the track on his day off and wear a green transparent stone in a gold ring'.(49) The victory of Richard Nixon at the Republican Convention is 'The apocalyptic hour of Uriah Heep'.(72)

Juxtaposed with these observations is an alternative reality which is defined in a postscript to the article.

> I was forcing a reality, I was bending reality like a field of space to curve the time I wished to create. I was not writing with the hope that perchance I could find reality by being sufficiently honest to perceive it, but on the contrary was distorting reality in the hope that thereby I could affect it . . . Whether I was right or wrong in fact may not be so important as its psychological reality in my own mind.(74–5)

Although the drama of the article does not explicitly characterise this psychological reality, it is clearly to be equated with the subterranean mythical reality that the protagonist attempts to define. In the description of the qualities of a political convention that are suggested to him on nominating day, a purpose and a design is discovered beneath the strident chaos. If a convention is 'a fiesta, a carnival, a pig-rooting, horse-snorting, band-playing, voice-screaming medieval get-together . . .' it is because 'our politics still smell of the bedroom and the kitchen, rather than having descended to us from the chill punctilio of aristocratic negotiation'.(66) This image of the origin of American politics manages to incorporate both the chaos and the hidden design, the corruption of political dealing and the 'subterranean' dreams and longings of a people that come together in Kennedy. Mailer successfully manages to suggest that the superficial reality of this Convention veils a 'real subterranean life'(38) which is discovered by a narrator who invades a 'No Man's Land . . .'.(37) This describes a point of view that evades the conventional political categories of Left, Right and Centre while simultaneously drawing from these categories in the course of the narrative.

The protagonist of 'Superman Comes to the Supermarket' distorts social reality in his report of the Democratic Convention because he hopes to correct, or at the least, expose the flaccidness of

American politics, which exists 'because opposing armies never meet'.(37) In his attempt to give the opposed realities, which his protagonist dramatises, a general social relevance, Mailer discusses minority groups in 'The Tenth Presidential Paper', specifically the American Jew and the American negro. Rather than aspire to integration with the uniform middle of American life, the member of a minority group should maintain his social alienation. He will then feel 'as if he possesses God and the Devil within himself, that the taste of his own death is already in his cells, that his purchase on eternity rises and falls with the calm or cowardice of his actions'.(206) There are obvious similarities, in this definition, with the existential hipster—notably the stress on immediate action whose end will be meaningful but mysterious. But, by taking discernible social groups to represent his minority, rather than creating a revolutionary group, Mailer includes the temptation to conform, the need for social endorsement which exists side by side with a rebellious psychological reality. The themes and the form of the pieces in *The Presidential Papers* and *Cannibals and Christians* are based upon this notion of opposing forces within the individual which maintain a creative communication. In 'An Impolite Interview' with Paul Krassner, Mailer will therefore decry the bombing of a village, not because the pilot found that the explosion of the bomb was beautiful but because the perception of this beauty is given priority over the helpless people killed. The conflict and potential destruction found in a boxing match, however, is endorsed by Mailer—even the match that resulted in the killing of Paret by Griffith—since it begins as an equal opposition and therefore allows for communication. By the same logic, Mailer has little sympathy, in 'The Tenth Presidential Paper', for the theory of surrealist art which joins opposite and irreconcilable notions and images, in order to demonstrate the destruction of communication. Although this is a kind of artistic destruction which accurately mirrors the foundation of modern existence built upon interruption and annoyance, it violates the premise which Mailer considers to be crucial to his work—' "that life is probably good . . ." '.(152) If it is not, then action is reduced to an absurdity.

Mailer conceives of this communication of opposed forces in his narrators very much in terms of the sparring encounter reminiscent of a boxing match. The balance of these oppositions that shapes his fiction is maintained like a prizefighter training for a match. He tells Steven Marcus that 'You develop consciousness as you grow older which enables you to write about anything, in effect, and write about it well. That is, provided you keep your consciousness in shape and don't relax into the flabby styles of thought which surround one everywhere'.(255) When Mailer employs his metaphorical oppositions to keep in shape, to flex his muscles; when he is using his fictional journalism to practise his manipulation of these entities, he loses sight of the literal states of mind (courage or moral growth for example) to which the best of his writing is committed to discovering. The definition that James Guetti gives of the cognitive metaphor illuminates this tendency of Mailer towards mere systematisation: ' . . . the consequent denial of this ability to know—a denial of cognitive powers with a proportional insistance upon imaginative complexity for its own sake and not as a means to an ineffable end—is of course the general parallel to the dissolution of metaphor itself'.[3] In 'Ten Thousand Words a Minute' which is an account of the fight between Sonny Liston and Floyd Patterson for the World Heavyweight Championship, Mailer seeks to establish a dramatic connection between this boxing match and the narrating reporter that attends the match, by stressing the power of Magic which he describes as an agent of both God and the Devil. It is a technique which transforms the narrator into a protagonist because the confrontation between Patterson and Liston is a metaphorically expressed psychological reality, which is endorsed by the social implications of the match that are assessed by a reporter.

On the afternoon of the fight, the narrator, along with several other reporters, goes to the Playboy Club. As they idly try to predict its outcome, their mood suddenly becomes charged with 'expectation, of omen and portent . . .' because 'God or the Devil or the agent of both, which is Magic, has entered his brain before an irrevocable battle'.(257) The uncertain relation of these forces to Patterson and Liston is quickly sensed by the commonsensical reporter who explains the intuition away in terms of his drinking and lack of sleep. He turns to an analysis of the social forces that are represented by Patterson and Liston, by examining the reactions of the negroes he has interviewed, and concludes that Patterson has the larger support because 'Floyd was the proof a man could be successful and yet be secure. If Liston won, the old torment was open again. A man could be successful *or* he could be secure. He could not have both'.(261) After establishing Patterson as the socially favoured contestant, the narrator can then return to his metaphorical entities which are clarified and corroborated by the information that the reporter has gathered. Patterson is 'the champion of every lonely adolescent and every man who had been forced to live alone . . . He was the hero of all those unsung romantics . . . He was the artist. He was the man who could not forgive himself if he gave less than his best chance for perfection'.(261) Liston, on the other hand, is 'the secret hero of every man who had ever given mouth to a final curse against the dispositions of the Lord and made a pact with Black Magic. Liston was Faust . . . He was the hero of . . . anyone who was fixed on power'.(262) The narrator is established as a protagonist because, as these convictions illustrate, he possesses a literally embattled perception as he approaches Comiskey Park in Chicago.

The account of the fight that begins with the description of the audience and ends with Patterson's dramatic defeat in the first round takes its form from the oscillation between the metaphorically expressed forces which emanate from within the narrator and the closely observed events which take place in front of him. The tension that results from these two points of view constitutes the plot of this fictionalised ceremony of violence. Comiskey Park is compared to the Colosseum, because 'arenas take on prehistoric breath at night . . .',(270) but then it loses its imaged grandeur as the reporter assesses the nature of the audience. The group of Mafia members, who are initially characterised by their vicious faces, are transformed into masters of magical art, who will shoot mental arrows into Patterson. This dramatic pace comes to a complete halt in the fourth section however when Mailer himself takes over from the narrator in order to examine the shocking elimination of Patterson in the first round. The metaphorical oppositions no longer emanate from the narrator, they cease to perform a dramatic function and are instead an arbitrary assemblage of terms that are self-consciously incongruous: 'Sex had proved superior to Love still one more time, the Hustler had taken another pool game from the Infantryman, the Syndicate rolled out the Liberal, the Magician hyped the Artist . . .'.(276) When Mailer goes on to add 'and, since there were more than a few who insisted on seeing them simply as God and the Devil', (ibid) he is apologising, and therefore undermining the drama of the narrator's intuitions, rather than corroborating them, as he intends. The repetition of these systematic oppositions, the announcement that prepares for, and intends to justify, Mailer's confrontation with Liston only serves to emphasise the loss of dramatic power and pace. 'I began . . . to see myself as some sort of center about which all that had been lost must now rally. It was not even simple insanity: it was a kind of metaphorical leap across a gap.' (282) That Mailer in fact made a fool of himself in this episode with Liston need not have detracted from the success of his writing. The example of Mailer's drunken performance at the Ambassador Theatre in Washington which was written about with dignity and passion in *The Armies of the Night* bears this out. What Mailer fails to do in the fourth section of 'Ten Thousand Words a Minute' is to create an objective point of view which will establish the dramatic relevance of his actions.

When they operate successfully, Mailer's metaphorical oppositions struggle to define an order or meaning out of a general condition of social decay and disease. The order is not of the kind that is controlled by immutable laws, since the terms of the metaphor change as the experience alters. Mailer pithily expresses this in a poem:

A Waltz

Paper covers rock
  rock breaks scissor
  scissor cuts paper

A woman can always
  take a man

A fag may always
  take a woman

A man may always
  take a fag

Circles bore me

They obey
  too many laws[4]

Mailer's metaphorical version of order suggests that there is a moral truth which is no less real because of its apparently paradoxical nature.

The character of John Kennedy in *The Presidential Papers* is alternatively depicted as a hero and a moral coward. This kind of dichotomy is a good illustration of the way that Mailer engages with, in order to struggle against the flow of public events. But it also reflects the conflict within the narrator which is the result of a deep disillusionment after his initial propagandising for Kennedy. He is a failed political candidate by the time that Kennedy has apparently endorsed the fiasco of the Bay of Pigs invasion of Cuba in 1961, and the two open letters, one dealing with this incident and one with the confrontation with Russia over Cuba in 1962, betray the full fury of his disillusionment. The letters argue the pointlessness of a conflict with Russia, the virtue of making Castro's Cuba an ally, but the core of the discussion lies in the advocation of a productive and creative conflict. A Cold War of ideologies that never meet but foster paranoid lies about the opposition is 'brutally stupid'(92); a war that only apparently stems from the Left and Right. In actual fact it is a symptom of the totalitarianism of society, the dead and apathetic Centre which wars against itself to no end. The second letter is interesting in that the writer assumes the right to some intimacy of tone after endorsing Kennedy's fight for the Presidency. The struggle to assess Kennedy's character, the uneasy admission of failure which nevertheless refuses to relinquish an uncertain and secret admiration of the President all corroborate the representative authority of the tone of address. There is a genuine struggle to establish immutable moral criteria which nevertheless must fail given the ambiguity of the issue. Kennedy displayed a strength in delivering his ultimatum to Krushchev yet it was a confrontation which he himself had unnecessarily provoked. Was Kennedy noble or nerveless? '. . . will you be the one to save us or to blow us up?' (124) In *Cannibals and Christians* (A Review of *JFK: The Man and the Myth* by Victor Lasky) Kennedy is described as having 'a character thus created of the most impossible ingredients for his venture: overweening ambition and profound political caution . . .'.(203) This dilemma dominates *The Presidential Papers*. It provokes Mailer's persona, the 'existential candidate', to seek new terms of conflict in place of the ones that Kennedy has provoked, while simultaneously stimulating a conflict within this persona between his admiration and censure of the President. In one sense, this stems from a fury that Kennedy the politician should prove to be so different from the hero that the narrator of 'Superman Comes to the Supermarket' had created. More importantly, however, it records the profound gap between individual thinking and public leadership or between myth and politics.

The force with which Mailer expresses his loathing for the

totalitarian form of life in America, and his conviction of the individual's ability to express himself freely in exciting and productive ways once this repressive force is overcome, is not the attitude of a man championing the masses, nor is it a simple confidence in the inherent virtue of the individual. To Mailer, the notion of grouping men together under the label 'the masses' is as repugnant as the operation of the mass-media, the proliferation of mass architecture, or the implementation of mass political programmes. It is a word that creates, not describes a reality; a word that does not describe a group so much as an attitude of mind that is so enslaved as to be formless. The theme that Mailer sounds again and again in the writing collected in *The Presidential Papers* and *Cannibals and Christians* is that America is suffering, but not from anything so concrete as an atrophy of Left or Right wing leadership. The death of Kennedy, the rise to power of Johnson, the race riots and acceleration of the Cold War and the war in Vietnam are effects rather than causes of a social breakdown. The social plague is found only in symptoms, undifferentiated architecture, viruses rather than diseases, jargon rather than language and inorganic plastic rather than organic wood. Mailer's search for a root cause to this state of general atrophy at first seems to deny the philosophy of Hip in 'The White Negro', which is 'to exist without roots',(271) to cast off 'the inefficient and often antiquated nervous circuits of the past . . .'.(277) In 'The Existential Heroine', he reacts to Jackie Kennedy's tour of the White House with the reflection: 'we have lost our past, we live in that airless no-man's-land of the perpetual present, and so suffer doubly as we strike into the future because we have no roots by which to project ourselves forward, or judge our trip'.(110) But Mailer is distinguishing between a conventional concept of history which denotes a past dominated by empty concepts and preconceptions, and a personalised history that is constantly recreated by the individual. It is the abnegation of personal responsibility that Mailer wishes to emphasise in his enumeration of a society that has divorced itself 'from the materials of the earth . . .',(173) from the senses, through fear.

There is a cultural conservatism governing the radicalism of the personalised history that the writers of the pieces in *The Presidential Papers* and *Cannibals and Christians* advocate. Yet the radical stance is not compromised by this conservatism when the performance of the writer demonstrates a fictional control over his material. Richard

Poirier launches an attack against Mailer's élitist abstractions'[5] which, he believes, stem from an 'obsessive fear of technology'.[6] The élitist concept of art and culture, he argues, is the only alternative that Mailer can find to the subtly overwhelming power of technology and, he concludes: 'Part of the fear of technology as expressed in the Shelleyan promotion of art and of the artist is really a fear among certain cultural élitists about the continued predominance of the written word, of literature, and of the edified past'.[7] Poirier is, like Hassan,[8] not arguing for an end to literature and the written word, but an end to the neurotic elevation of culture by those critics and writers who do not have the resources to conduct their own eloquent defence against forces they do not understand and therefore abuse. As such, it is a brave and extreme stance that he is taking.

Poirier's attack against Mailer is justified. Modern science is the scapegoat that is blamed for the social plague that is defined throughout these two collections. Towards the end of the 1960s, when he collected *Cannibals and Christians*, Mailer wrote of scientists who had transferred their insight derived from poetic vision and culture to that of methodological experiment; from revealing nature to converting it. Mailer counters this social epidemic by advocating the 'danger' of metaphor, where 'contradictory meanings collect too easily about the core of meaning; unconnected meanings connect themselves'. He is against a 'rabidity of experiment, a fetichism of experiment'.(349) But this is acceptable only if these contradictory and unconnected meanings are presented as a fluid performance on the part of the writer. When Mailer extols the nature and status of art and the artist to the extent that these contradictions are hardly figurative, then he is, like the scientist, converting nature, rather than revealing it. The contradictory nature of the truth that Mailer's writing struggles to define makes a question that James Guetti poses on the unstable nature of the metaphorically expressed reality particularly pertinent to Mailer: 'One is constantly forced to consider and to determine the point at which an expression of failure or near failure becomes a failure of expression . . . that is, by presenting the idea of a fundamental incoherence in experience, the novel itself may become incoherent'.[9] When Mailer's use of metaphor simply furthers or gratuitously creates an ambiguity, the connection between the writer and his subject matter becomes a fanciful one and the moral point of his argument is weakened.

This is illustrated in a fictional interview that all but concludes *Cannibals and Christians*, called 'The Political Economy of Time'. Mailer theorises on the nature of form, and in a long preamble he elucidates in some detail how the artist defines his existence and actively formulates his creation. Temporarily leaving aside the metaphorical conceits by which the dialogue proceeds, the emphasis is continually upon the precariousness of artistic creation, the absence of aesthetic criteria, the recalcitrance of environment (in the most general sense) to which the artist must turn for his subject matter. 'Form . . . is the record of a war . . . the detailed record of an engagement' that 'hints at the move from potential to actual'.(413–14) To the extent to which this constitutes a good working theory by which Mailer's persona approaches his subject matter and consolidates the form of his argument by converting this warring form into 'the physical equivalent of memory',(415) it is an acceptable hypothesis. In terms of the metaphorical structure of the dialogue, the war is described as a metaphysical battle between God and the Devil. In 1958, Mailer had described to Richard Stern his belief that God was not an all-powerful force but an embattled and fallible Being struggling for supremacy against a Devil whose evil was manifest in the growing uniformity of American society. Mailer comes as near as he has ever done in this interview to expressing a sincerely felt metaphysical reality. In 'The Political Economy of Time', he makes the mistake of trying simultaneously to employ his concept of a grand metaphysical battle as a literally held belief and as a means to advance his aesthetic theories.

It is a mistake because the reader is then forced into a close questioning of the logic of the argument as a metaphysical speculation, while Mailer is simultaneously demanding that the reader must accept the presence of ambiguities and contradictions, since the purpose of metaphor is to counteract the precise methodology to which science has made man subject. If God embodies everything that moves towards growth and potential fulfilment in the search for a satisfactory—that is dynamic—form, the Devil is waste: that is, institutional life, mass communication and uniformity. If this is an apparently simple opposition, it nevertheless more than suffices for the exercise of Mailer's talent. But it is not possible to argue in Mailer's case, as can be done in that of Blake's, Yeats' and Lawrence's for example, that the artist's private system is immune from a close logical scrutiny if it is suitably transmuted, in the poem or novel, into an image or set of images that metaphorically illuminate certain verities of the human condition.

Since Mailer consolidates a persona in the writing included in these two collections, that not only metaphorically embodies this God–Devil conflict, but, on occasion, assumes that it be interpreted literally, the reader is forced to ask that if life is basically good, if God is the rightful owner of the world by virtue of His creation, then from where does the Devil originate? Does evil emanate from the fact that God shares His fallible nature with man and is therefore as much subject to the abuse of his creation? Or is the Devil an independent force? The 'interviewer' asks Mailer, 'Is this plague equal to the Devil?' and Mailer replies 'Again I have no idea. Perhaps it wishes to destroy the Devil along with everything else. Perhaps the Devil bears the same relation to the plague that Faust bears to Mephisto'.(407) The 'interviewer's' mocking criticism: 'What you have stated up to here is so obviously a philosophy of hugely paranoid proportions'(409) is unsatisfactory because Mailer is deliberately obfuscating the terms by which his theories may be interpreted, by furthering confusion rather than discovering an ambiguity that already exists. Is then a man a machine because of individual weakness, that leads to a failure to resist his science-dominated society, or because of a malignant external force? There is a similar problem in an article called 'In the Red Light', which is included in *Cannibals and Christians* and which reports on the Republican Convention of 1964. The narrating reporter insists on discerning metaphorically expressed forces that are blatantly uncorroborated by the events or participants. The mood of a possible apocalyptic disaster is established in a short opening section which is headed by a quotation from *The Day of the Locust* by Nathanael West. It consists of a part-imaginary, part-reported conversation in an aeroplane on the sickness of the American nation. Mailer introduces the refrain of the article: 'was the country extraordinary or accursed?'(22) through a persona called Quentin Compson. By referring here to the tortured and introspective character in William Faulkner's novel, *The Sound and the Fury*, Mailer intends to dramatise the potential madness involved in the pursuit of such a question.

In order to discover the enigma of America's fate however, it is a reporter who focuses his attention upon Barry Goldwater as the most powerful figure in the race for the nomination. But from the reporter's portrayal of the Goldwater supporters to the description of his family, his headquarters and finally Goldwater himself: 'Half-

Jew and blue-eyed—if you belonged in the breed, you knew it was manic-depressive for sure: a man who designed his own electronic flagpole to raise Old Glory at dawn, pull her down at dusk . . .',(59) there is no satisfactory dramatic correlative to the refrain. The reporter admits his boredom so that although his inner debate as to whether communism existed as a real threat or whether America could not survive without an economy geared to war is a sincerely and provocatively expressed problem, the Republican Convention is patently neither extraordinary nor accursed. The reporter attempts to make Goldwater an integral part of his own psychic reality in order to give him a necessary status: 'Indeed I knew that Goldwater could win because something in me leaped at the thought; a part of me, a devil, wished to take that choice'.(59) But nothing Goldwater says or does corroborates this intuition. Similarly, when the reporter insists that, despite the nominal boredom of the proceedings, it would remain 'one of the most important [conventions] in our history' for it offered to the press and television 'four days of anxiety as pure and deep as a child left alone in a house',(43–4) there is no corresponding evocation of pure and deep anxiety in the events described. The reporter must digress in order to explain the retaliation of the frustrated Right which will succeed the outbreak of the beat generation, of which he sees signs at this Convention. What is lacking is not information, nor are the reporter's speculations untenable. The relationship between Mailer and his narrator is uneasy, which prevents him from successfully fictionalising his material.

Mailer is at his best when he manages to establish a satisfactory correlative between his persona, the issues, and figures that personify those issues. When this is achieved, the performance of his persona, which engages national events, issues and leaders with authority and familiarity, makes a direct appeal to a society of individuals, not a society of groups. Accordingly, the persona in these collections assumes that he is a microcosm arguing for the existence of fundamental and universal verities of the human macrocosm. Mailer goes on to argue in 'An Impolite Interview':

if you assume that life is good, then you have to assume that those things which keep life from happening—which tend to make life more complex without becoming more useful, more stimulating—are bad.

> Anything that tends to make a man a machine without giving
> him the power to increase the real life in himself is bad.(152)

Real life, which is good, is therefore an inherent force in human
nature, but it can only become an active principle by a self-
conscious antagonism toward synthetic machine-life, which is bad.
Fulfilment, growth and goodness are all words used to express the
positive states of life which are constantly in a state of becoming and
which are defined by those negative forces which seek to destroy
these states.

If Mailer's reaction to the administrations of Kennedy and
Johnson sets the theme of *The Presidential Papers* and *Cannibals and
Christians*, there is another figure whom he has elevated to the status
of an exiled saviour and whose image dominates both of these
collections: that of Ernest Hemingway. Mailer has long admired
Hemingway; in a postscript to the 'Advertisement' for *The Deer
Park*, he extolled the older writer's famous code of action by which
one's creative talents exist in proportion to one's active courage. No
matter how unlike the work of these two men is (and the strenuous
gymnastics of Mailer's prose could not exist in a more direct
opposition than to Hemingway's stylistic economy), Hemingway is
important and admirable to Mailer since he is a writer whose ideals
are uncompromised despite obvious human weaknesses, and whose
entrenched literary status, despite the self-imposed exile, is un-
shaken. For it is the nature of the writer, the artist—not the reporter,
the speech-maker or political pundit—with which Mailer is
concerned and which he offers as a real alternative to the plague-
ridden society about which he writes. His purpose in collecting his
pieces together in these two volumes is to establish a consistent and
viable theme which will give each book a satisfactory aesthetic
unity. *The Presidential Papers* begins and ends with the writer
defining existential politics. In the Prefatory Paper, he specifies that
social disease springs from ideas in power without a leader to
embody them. Existential politics is then rooted in the concept of
the hero, who is 'a consecutive set of brave and witty self-creations'.
(16) At the book's conclusion, the 'brave and witty self-creations'
are no longer attributable to Kennedy but to the writer. In his
performance throughout the book, it is he, not the President, who
has constructed 'the few hypotheses by which we guide ourselves
only by drawing into ourselves the instinctive logic our inner voice
tells us is true to the relations *between* mysteries'.(291)

Cannibals and Christians is framed by the image of a metal GULF sign. In his opening Argument, Mailer laconically explains that the GULF sign was considered by himself and a group of friends, as a possible pop-art object in the height of fashionable, intellectual taste. It is finally left to rust on the beach near the spot where it was found. But the sign symbolises, for Mailer, an ambiguous artistic symptom of technological society, which he goes on to call the art of the absurd. His discussion in this Argument is a logical progression from his declared suspicion of surrealist art in 'The Tenth Presidential Paper'. Is absurdist art a symptom of social breakdown or does it serve to expose and thereby 'rescue civilization from the pit and plague of its bedding . . .'?(16) In his final Argument, the GULF sign is reinstated as Mailer reflects upon this enigma: 'some art movements serve to wash out the sludge of civilization, some leave us deeper in the pit. The art of the absurd is here to purify us or to swamp us—we do not know . . .'.(348) This issue stresses Mailer's ambivalence and anxiety about his position as a creative artist in a society that can utilise the instant products of its technology as art objects. The writer in *Cannibals and Christians* constantly seeks for some means of satisfactory communication—both in his own performance and between himself and his ailing society.

Hemingway's death, apparently by an act of suicide, confirmed for Mailer the impossibly high price the writer must pay if he is to maintain his convictions and continue to believe in his talent in spite of the judgement of his public. It would seem that the exiled image of Hemingway became inextricably mixed with Mailer's struggle to write and publish *The Deer Park*, so that, after Hemingway's suicide, after Mailer's retreat from fiction into fictional journalism, death became synonymous with daring social acrimony. His brilliant and moving column in *The Presidential Papers*, on Hemingway's death, in which he denied the term suicide even though the old man undeniably shot himself, concludes: 'If we are ill and yet want to go on, we must put up the ante. If we lose, it does not mean we wished to die'.(118) In 'Some Children of the Goddess', death is the literal or mental limbo that follows the artist's struggle of integrity with a society that cannot be ignored: 'If a writer is really good enough and bold enough he will, by the logic of society, write himself out onto the end of a limb which the world will saw off. He does not go necessarily to his death, but he must dare it'.(136) The tragic irony which the death of Hemingway embodied and which, to Mailer, threatens any dedicated writer, is that once society has accepted and established his literary status, the death which he must constantly dare is enacted against himself. It is a battle of nerves which will eventually end in his physical death. In *The Presidential Papers*, Mailer used the figure of Hemingway in his open letter to Fidel Castro, to suggest that only a man with literary status could mollify America's antipathy to Cuba: 'The world will read what Hemingway has to say, the world will read it critically, because he will be making a history, he may even be preparing a ground on which you and our new President can meet'.(89)

The persona of these two collections is only incidentally known to the world as a novelist; he is first and foremost a literary exhibitionist and talented journalist. But to Mailer, the writer, if not necessarily a novelist, is a creative artist, despite the radical adjustments he might make to the conventional definition of this appellation. In *The Presidential Papers* and *Cannibals and Christians* he uses Hemingway as a recognisable image of the kind of artist he considers himself to be. After each of these collections was published, Mailer went on to write a novel. The effort required was enormous, since Mailer chose to eschew a conflict with conventional social reality and, like Hemingway in the final years of his life, conduct an internal battle against the self's 'wild dirty little dwarf'(310) which is Mailer's personification of the id or antisocial impulse in his fictional interview, 'The Metaphysics of the Belly'. Since this reduces the possibility of expressing and controlling the emotions of the writer by enacting the battle between the man of 'magnificent senses' and the dwarf who wants only to kill the writer (ibid), there is a great deal at stake. The opposing inner tensions that Stephen Rojack in *An American Dream* struggles to elucidate enact this crucial internal battle. As Rojack fights for a true sense of himself, his sexual activity represents Mailer's fight for the status of the creative artist.

In this respect, *An American Dream* is a direct development of 'The Time of Her Time' where Sergius O'Shaugnessy's sexual conquest of Denise Gondelman is a metaphor for Mailer's creative will. But the will which is enacted in the short story is imaginatively creative in the broadest fictional sense: it belongs to the essayist, columnist and journalist. Rojack's sexual activities, however, are the metaphorical activities of the novelist. The return to the senses which he reaches for and which finally slip his grasp, are the 'magnificent senses' of the individual as novelist whose courage alone can effectively counter the entropic waste of society. Mailer concludes

'Some Children of the Goddess', his paper on contemporary fiction, by arguing:

> A war has been fought by some of us over the last fifteen years to open the sexual badlands to our writing, and that war is in the act of being won. Can one now begin to think of an attack on the stockade—those dead forts where the spirit of twentieth-century man, frozen in flop and panic before the montage of his annihilation, has collected, like castrated cattle behind the fence? Can the feet of those infantrymen of the arts, the novelists, take us through the mansions and the churches into the palace of the Bitch where the real secrets are stored? We are the last of the entrepreneurs, and one of us homeless guns had better make it, or the future will smell like the dead air of the men who captured our time during that huge collective cowardice which was the aftermath of the Second War.(161)

Stephen Rojack is most obviously that type of Maileresque character who combines, in agonising conflict, the heroic qualities of the individualist with the roles of the conventional, social mass man. Because he has the courage to explore into himself, as individualist, he discovers an intuitive relationship between his self and his surroundings which is governed by his heightened senses. Rojack characterises this as the operation of magical forces in terms that are identical to those in which the reporter-narrator becomes part of the Liston–Patterson World Heavyweight Championship fight in 'Ten Thousand Words a Minute'. The reporter states that:

> All of one's small actions became significant. It is not madness exactly . . . If the World is a war between God and the Devil, and Destiny is the line of battle, then a general may be permitted to think that God or the Devil or the agent of both, which is Magic, has entered his brain before an irrevocable battle(257)

Immediately after he murders Deborah, Rojack goes into the bathroom and experiences a heightening of the senses similar to the effect of peyote. Finally, he regards his reflected image:

> My hair was alive and my eyes had the blue of a mirror held between the ocean and the sky—they were eyes to equal at last the eyes of the German who stood before me with a bayonet . . . I

looked deeper into the eyes in the mirror as if they were keyholes
to a gate which gave on a palace, and asked myself, 'Am I now
good? Am I evil for ever?'[10]

Both the reporter and Rojack demonstrate a measure of courage in
facing up to the authority of the senses. They recognise that the
senses provide no simple criteria with which to assess experience
but, rather, that they deepen its ambiguity. This ambiguity, for
both characters, is expressed in their preoccupation with death. The
reporter, in 'Ten Thousand Words a Minute', remembers the fight
between Paret and Griffith which he attended and describes, with
sad but respectful nostalgia, the death of Paret in the ring. Contrary
to popular opinion, the reporter argues that it is not shocking that
the killing occurred, because (along with Hemingway) he feels that
'it belonged to his (the boxer's) ability to create art and artful
movement on the edge of death or pain or danger or attack, and it
had much to say about the subtleties of human style'.(268) Death
under these conditions is 'more alive than life'(ibid)—it comes at
the end of a life which is lived as an exploration into, and acceptance
of, the mystery of death.

During the war, Rojack attacks and kills singlehanded a group of
Germans entrenched behind a machine gun, which earns him the
DSC. In attacking and shooting the first three, the possibility of his
own death balances with the deaths of the Germans in an equality of
combat similar to the 'style' of the boxing match, because Rojack
considers death 'as a possibility considerably more agreeable than
my status in some further disorder'.(10) He is 'ready to die in
atonement . . .'.(11) When he faces the fourth German, however,
this awareness deserts him: 'suddenly it was all gone, the clean
presence of *it*, the grace, *it* had deserted me . . .'.(13) Rojack has
lost the courage that is necessary in order to trust the authority of his
senses. But the vision in the eyes of the German soldier haunts him:
'I could have had a career in politics if only I had been able to think
that death was zero, death was everyone's emptiness. But I knew it
was not'.(15) Rojack only begins to rebuild his self when he kills
Deborah; when his eyes are 'equal at last'(45) to those of the
German soldier. It is the creative self, the will that Mailer evoked in
'The White Negro', 'it' being 'God; not the God of the Churches but
the unachievable whisper of mystery within sex . . .',(283) and
which he used as a metaphor for his own artistic will in 'The Time of
Her Time': 'a Village stickman who could muster enough of the

divine It on the head of his will to call forth more than one becoming out of the womb of feminine Time . . .'.(409)

As Rojack has his hands on Deborah's throat, he compares his feeling of impending release to a heaven of 'some quiver of jewelled cities shining in the glow of a tropical dust . . .'.(38) His act of strangling Deborah becomes inextricably intermingled with his imaginative evocation of this image so that, as he presses harder on her throat, he is in fact 'driving now with force against that door' (ibid) which is concealing the heavenly city from him. This is an image which prophesies the value of his lovemaking with Cherry: 'I was passing through a grotto of dark lights, like coloured lanterns beneath the sea, a glimpse of that quiver of jewelled arrows, that heavenly city which had appeared as Deborah was expiring in the lock of my arm . . .'.(131) Balanced against these two images of Heaven are two visions of Hell. After his sexual marathon with Ruta, Rojack has 'a vision . . . of a huge city in the desert, in some desert, was it a place on the moon? For the colours had the unreal pastel of a plastic and the main street was flaming with light at five a.m. A million light bulbs lit the scene'.(52) This prophesies the city that Rojack finally sees on the horizon when he speaks to Cherry in Heaven from a disused telephone booth. Since he wanders into the desert from Las Vegas verging on a complete breakdown, the city is part of a Hellish rather than a Heavenly landscape. Although Rojack is finally 'not good enough'(271) to eliminate the waste, the arid emptiness of American society, Mailer is able to enact, through his novelist's imagination, the possibility of personal and, by implication, social redemption.

That *An American Dream* ends on a note of wry resignation is a demonstration of Mailer's determination to minimise the liar that he insists is at the centre of every novelist. Mailer cannot allow the vision of salvation, expressed by Rojack as he makes love to Cherry, to be more than potential because, as he has seriously and eloquently argued in 'Some Children of the Goddess', the novel has been unavoidably weakened in its ability to provide a social corrective. 'Literature then had failed. The work was done by the movies, by television. The consciousness of the masses and the culture of the land trudged through endless mud'.(128) The progression of Rojack from his marriage to Deborah, through the single encounter with Ruta to the promise of mutual love and long-term happiness with Cherry, is described by him in a series of metaphors that corresponds precisely to Mailer's own metaphorical system, expounded in *Advertisements for Myself*, developed in 'The Metaphysics of the Belly' and 'The Political Economy of Time' and adapted here to chart his own development as a novelist.

The threat and challenge that Deborah poses for Rojack are nothing less than a metaphorical expression of Mailer's grim determination to tackle the role of novelist after a long period of intimidation. Deborah is 'a great bitch, a lioness of the species: unconditional surrender was her only raw meat . . . For ideally a Great Bitch delivers extermination to any bucko brave enough to take carnal knowledge of her'.(16) In 'Some Children of the Goddess', which was written just as he was beginning to work on *An American Dream*, Mailer characterises the novel as a Great Bitch. She is vicious, powerful, demanding but, above all, admirable. She demands a cruel but just initiation from all those with creative pretentions:' "Man, I made her moan", goes the cry of the young writer. But the Bitch laughs afterward in her empty bed. "He was so sweet in the beginning", she declares, "but by the end he just went, 'Peep, peep, peep' ".'(134) The murder of Deborah, the Great Bitch, is therefore a necessary initiation of courage for Rojack before he can claim to act on the authority of his senses. Being with Deborah, Rojack is imbued with wit, vitality, stamina, style: 'It was just that the gift was only up for loan'.(26) His impotence leaves him stranded between two extremes: 'Living with her [Deborah] I was murderous; attempting to separate, suicide came into me'.(17) Murder will enable Rojack to appropriate that strength; suicide will destroy the self for not possessing that strength. Before he gains the necessary courage, he has to experience the nadir of selfhood. If the Great Bitch does not acknowledge that she needs him, then Rojack's power has truly disappeared: 'I had opened a void—I was now without centre. Can you understand? I did not belong to myself any longer. Deborah had occupied my centre'.(34) After killing her, he returns to a sense of self-possession: 'I was as far into myself as I had ever been and the universes wheeled in a dream'.(39)

The result of his repossession of the self is the integration of forces which had previously operated at odds with one another and had therefore based his personality upon a void. The result of this integration is to prevent Rojack from calling the police and to propel him downstairs, where he embarks upon a sexual marathon with Deborah's German maid, Ruta. It is, though, a precarious integration that can just as easily become an alienation from the self. Rojack alternately enters Ruta's vagina and anus, but it is a highly self-conscious act that all but eliminates Ruta as a separate entity. The imagery he evokes recalls his earlier dilemma of being caught between murder and suicide, between a tropical fecundity and a desert of sterility. Ruta's womb is 'that deserted warehouse on the moon' whereas her anus is full of 'pirate's gold'.(51) Rojack then goes on to establish the dialectic of his actions in a system of metaphors that Mailer uses in *Cannibal and Christians* to describe the 'double sense of identity'(101) of his narrators. These metaphorical oppositions are either employed in a scatological context (the vagina and the anus or the mouth and the anus denoting fertility and waste) or a metaphysical context (good and evil which again refers to creation and destruction). Similarly, Rojack moves from the Devil to the Lord, the earth to the sea, and with every movement, he replenishes the sterility of Ruta's womb. As she says ' "I can make a baby now" '(ibid) Rojack is hard at work on the resourcefulness of his imagery, after his brief recourse to direct metaphorical opposition. Ruta's womb is 'a chapel now, with a few flowers in garden, a modest decent place, too modest perhaps for me, but its walls were snug, its odours were green, there was a sweetness in the chapel, a muted reverential sweetness in those walls of soft stone'.(52) As 'the fires' of the Devil continue to tempt Rojack, he no longer knows in which direction to turn his creative activity, and on a confused impulse, directs his orgasm toward the 'cellar' of Ruta's anus. When the detached ingenuity of Rojack's style (verbal and active) has terminated, however, its dialectic imposes a forced alienation from the self. 'Was that the cloud of oppression which had come to me in the dark? That the seed was expiring in the wrong field?'(55)

Rojack's need to find a permanently fertile place for that seed of creativity reaches a potential fulfilment in Cherry. After verbal foreplay in the nightclub, they make love in her Lower East Side retreat. A power returns to Rojack that he has inherited from Deborah, and, initially, this hatred is directed towards a comparatively self-absorbed effort to create an integrated identity. With Cherry, however, he finds he can abandon his self-conscious mental constructions and allow the act itself to guide him: 'we paid our devotions in some church no larger than ourselves . . .'.(130) When Cherry voluntarily makes it possible for her to conceive, Rojack is for the first time confidently directing his creativity—his seed— toward a possibility of growth. Cherry is a willing partner and not an antagonist.

There is, however, another equally important dimension to *An American Dream*. In his fictional journalism, Mailer's protagonists had dramatically appropriated, and often parodied, the public figures and their surroundings by means of a prose style that exposed the nature of their public performance. Mailer's developing fascination in the quality of the acting of any figure in the public eye is evidenced, in 'Superman Comes to the Supermarket' in his characterisation of Kennedy as a box office actor, and his delight at describing the obvious lack of Nixon's talent in accepting the Republican nomination. ' "Yes, I want to say," said Nixon, "that whatever abilities I have, I got from my mother." A tired pause . . . dull moment of warning, " . . . and my father". The connection now is made, the rest comes easy, " . . . and my school and my church" '.(58) The language of these performances is important to Mailer because it is the language of recognised power, which seeks to change a situation by controlling it. But, until he wrote *An American Dream*, Mailer had dramatised the nature of these acted performances through a protagonist who was both spectator and commentator. In his novel, he performs himself, through a series of voices that objectively view Rojack's consciousness. Mailer intends that these voices should parody the social milieu they apparently represent. Rojack's confrontations with his several antagonists in the course of the novel therefore represent the protagonist's consciousness as an amalgam of Rojack-and-Shago Martin, Rojack-and-Barney Oswald Kelly, Rojack-and-Lieutenant Roberts. These confrontations control the development of his identity, which then dictates the form of his social milieu. Mailer can enforce this transition without qualification, because on this level the writer's imagination is in complete control.

By turning his attention from John Kennedy, as an embodiment of the renaissance myth to Stephen Rojack, Mailer can control and eliminate the discrepancy between the mythical image of his renaissance man and the conventional reality which denies it. If, as he argues in 'Superman Comes to the Supermarket', 'the life of politics and the life of myth had diverged too far'(54), it was the novel that would rediscover a hero 'central to his time, a man whose personality might suggest contradictions and mysteries which would reach into the alienated circuits of the underground . . .'.(55) Yet Mailer was not reverting to his evasive insular definition of fiction expounded in the late 1950s. Stephen Rojack personifies the renaissance myth which is being ironically undermined by Mailer.

Northrop Frye defines the ironic myth 'as a parody of romance: the application of romantic mythical forms to a more realistic content which fits them in unexpected ways'.[11] Mailer begins his novel by listing the credentials of Rojack in a manner that is difficult to take seriously. Not only does Rojack boast an early intimacy with John Kennedy; he has gone on to become war hero, congressman, academic and television personality. These are enumerated with the casual air of the cliché because Rojack, locked in his ambiguous intuitions of magic and dread, remains an actor in his public roles. He embarks upon a quest, initiated by his murder of Deborah, the goal of which is to integrate his separate selves. This is not with a view to eliminating either the self belonging to the senses or the public image that is intellectually maintained. The two should coexist in a creative dialectic, like Mailer's opposing metaphorical entities.

When Rojack murders Deborah, he experiences a temporary integration, which prevents him from calling the police. Yet when he is attempting to wrest Cherry from the company of second-rate hoodlums, he has lost the ability to trust the authority of his senses. Mailer mocks the gravity with which Rojack describes his psychic warfare:

> the lights dimmed . . . either in fact or in the centre of my imagination, and I said to myself, 'Yes, you certainly will be dead in three days'. . . . Sitting where I was, not fifteen feet from the bar, I had come to the conclusion that if I were to be dead in three days, Romeo was the man who was likely to do the job. I had no idea if this thought came from what was most true in my instinct, or if my mind was simply sodden with idiocies.(107–8)

After Rojack is subjected to a particularly intense interrogation by Lieutenant Roberts, however, he again understands and experiences the wholeness of self. The secret of sanity is 'the ability to hold the maximum of possible combinations in one's mind, Robert's red pins on the precinct map and a paragraph from the middle of the Clark Reed Powell Prize Lecture: *On the Primitive View of Mystery*'.(162)

Rojack's moments of illumination are undermined, however, by the fact that he cannot control this oscillation between the brain and the senses. He has no choice as to which part of the self shall dictate his actions. The form of this bewildered and often agonised quest is an archetypal one. The hero must ascend from an inferno-like region, after a formal initiation and with a talisman (Shago Martin's umbrella) to a final confrontation with a demonic being. This ascent from Harlem and Shago Martin to the Waldorf Tower and Barney Oswald Kelly is the ascent from 'the buried gaming rooms of the unconscious to the tower of the brain'.(47) While Stephen Rojack is following this archetypal pattern in a quest for integration of the self, Mailer is demonstrating, through his resourceful characterisation of Martin and Kelly, that although Rojack has lost the power to choose, he, Mailer, has not. When Rojack confronts these two men in a battle for power, Mailer's verbal pyrotechnics effect a synthesis between his protagonist and antagonist. Mailer's purpose, in this presentation of Rojack's consciousness, is a satirical one. To return to the definition of Northrop Frye: 'Satire demands at least a token fantasy, a content which the reader recognizes as grotesque, and at least an implicit moral standard, the latter being essential in a militant attitude to experience'.[12] Both Shago Martin and Barney Kelly are grotesques in the sense that Mailer is carrying his knowledge of the type they represent and the role they play in his quest form to the extreme of caricature. They each personify within Rojack opposing forces which are struggling for dominance. Since they are the creation of Mailer's satirical exuberance, these characters are gigantic in their verbal performances.

When Martin intrudes into the momentary haven that Rojack and Cherry have created for themselves, the struggle for the right to enter Cherry's bed is of secondary importance in the confrontation between the two men. The primary issue is Rojack's fear and rejection of that part of himself personified by Martin. The fusion of the two men who are only apparently separate entities, is sardonically suggested by Martin, who describes himself as ' "a lily-white devil in a black ass"',(191) as being ' "a captive of white shit now . . ." '.(194) He is an overwhelmingly threatening figure and Rojack can only summon the courage to defy him when he feels 'an emptiness in his [Shago's] mood which I could enter'.(189) The implications of this fusion terrify and repel Rojack however and Mailer uses a sexual metaphor in order to stress this repulsion. Rojack physically attacks Martin who has taunted him with the words, ' "Up your ass, professor . . ." '.(195) Even as he is being crushed against the floor, he calls Rojack a bugger and utters his defiance by repeating the words ' "Up your ass" '. With Rojack's arms around Martin, their fighting stance takes on an ambiguous air when it is accompanied by this verbal defiance and which Rojack comes to acknowledge: 'when I got a whiff of his odour which had something of defeat in it, and a smell of full nearness as if we'd been in bed for an hour—well, it was too close: I threw him down the stairs'.(196) Rojack pays a high price for his wilful repulsion of Martin. Being unable to acknowledge and therefore understand the intuitive part of himself, he not only places the safety of Cherry in jeopardy, but reduces himself to the status of a wholly manipulated being. As the forces of Harlem and the Waldorf Tower converge within Rojack, he reflects: 'Did it matter where I went? . . . I would meet something tonight—was that not the odds? And the voice again: "Still it would have been better to choose" .'(206)

Despite his physical defeat, Martin maintains his power of choice. He is a talented jazz singer whose variety of styles find form in the control he exerts upon them. The 'snakes' in the 'tropical garden'(184) of his songs correspond to the tropical fecundity of the city of Rojack's imagination, after his murder of Deborah and his lovemaking with Cherry. Even Rojack, who belies his cowardice by remarking that 'His talent was too extreme', is aware that there is 'something complex in his style, some irony, some sense of control, some sense of the way everything is brought back at last under control'.(ibid) Martin's dazzling verbal performance, which captivates and controls both Rojack and Cherry from the moment he enters her room, is a brilliant demonstration, on the part of Mailer, of his ability to capture the style of a succession of voices. Martin is high on heroin, and by employing an astonishing range of language and tone of voice, he demonstrates how the meanings of his songs are found in the context in which they are sung. Mailer's presentation of Martin in this chapter is, in fact, an illustration of his discussion on the language of Hip in 'The White Negro'. Martin expects his songs to be interpreted, not by literally defining the words, but by relying on the 'nuance' of his voice which 'uses the nuance of the situation to convey the subtle contextual difference'. (281) Martin's belligerent yet amused assertion

'it's all shit, man except for the way I use it cause I let each accent pick its note, every tongue on a private note, when I sing it's a congregation of tongues, that's the spook in my music, that's why they got to buy me big or not at all, I'm not intimate, I'm Elizabethan, a chorus, dig?'(193)

is the culmination of a highly self-conscious and entertaining performance of a dazzling array of voices that reflect the society that wishes to patronise him and which he despises.

Martin begins by addressing Rojack in a voice that duplicates the enraged hip Negro, even while he is nominating Rojack as the ' "coonass blackass nigger jackaboo . . ." '.(187) But his succession of roles accelerates, as Rojack observes that 'Accents flew in and out of his speech like flying peacocks and bats'.(189) Martin's 'spasm of language . . .'(191) literally overwhelms Rojack by its sheer virtuosity. He spurns the ' "Village shit" ' and the ' "Mob shit" ' in favour of the ' "Society shit" '(192) because he knows that by exposing its hypocrisy, he is finding Rojack's weakest spot. Rojack's initial reaction to the entry of Martin is his memory of the latter's contemptuous rejection of Deborah's attempt to patronise him. It is this event which Martin has in mind, as he impersonates Deborah's voice, and then performs his own mocking social accomplishments.

'Cause I can do the tongues, all that cosmopolitan *dreck*, bit of French, bit of Texas, *soupçon* of Oxford jazz—I promise you;' he interpolated with a perfect London voice, 'that we'll have masses of fun and be happy as a clam, why', he said, snapping his fingers, 'I can pick up on German, Chinese, Russian (*Tovarich*, mother-sucker) I can do a piece of each little bit, St Nickolas Avenue *upper* nigger, Jamaican, Japanese, Javanese, high yaller sass—I just call on my adenoids, my fat lips and tonsils, *waaaaah*, I can do a *grande dame*, anything from a gasbag to Tallulah Bankhead, "*Out*, you pederast" . . .'.(193)

Like Martin, Barney Oswald Kelly is an actor with a perfect control over the roles he enacts. Mailer traces in more detail Kelly's progression from the elegant bereaved father-in-law to the corrupt 'big foul cat, carnal as the meat on a butcher's block'(219) who attempts to murder Rojack. Just as Rojack had been confronted with and repelled by the fusion with Martin, so he is horrified by a similar threat from Kelly. The burning air and the sense of inanimate death of Kelly's Waldorf apartment corresponds to the desertlike sterility that despoils the city of Rojack's vision after his lovemaking with Ruta. Although both men are ostensibly locking in a struggle over the memory of Deborah, she is, like Cherry, only a secondary issue in their confrontation. The powerful embrace that Kelly initially gives Rojack is a foretaste of their intimacy in the library with the Lucchese bed surrounded by baroque decadence. When Kelly describes his incest with Deborah, he reincarnates a lust for all three of Rojack's women:

> suddenly I knew what it had been like with Cherry and him, not so far from Ruta and me, no, not so far, and knew what it had been like with Deborah and him, what a hot burning two-backed beast, and I could hear what he offered now. Kelly wanted Ruta along, I could feel it like odour, he wanted the three of us on that Lucchese bed to lick and tear and spit and squat, roll and grovel, gorge each other in a disembowelment of sex for this Lucchese had been the bed where Kelly went off with Deborah to the tar-pits of the moon.(256)

It is at this moment that the two men merge, in the sense that Rojack is forced to recognise that the evil that Kelly embodies is the evil within himself. His despairing rejection of the knowledge, that both Kelly and Martin personify the brain–senses dichotomy within himself, prompts his reluctant decision to walk the parapet of Kelly's balcony, a trial of courage that he has fought against since he entered the apartment.

The parapet not only represents the boundary between a political (Kelly) and a demonised (Martin) ordering of reality, as Tony Tanner argues.[13] It can also be the boundary between the systematised but ambiguous dichotomy within the self and the purely theoretical, unexplored and therefore formless version of the self: 'promiscuous, reasonable, blind to the reach of the seas'.(257) Like the earlier scene on a balcony, Rojack is tempted to fly out into space with the deluded notion that only its freedom and emptiness can offer true oblivion to the embattled forces within him. It is because Rojack precariously balances on the edge between these two versions of himself, because he cannot summon the courage to commit himself to either extreme, that he fails Cherry. Kelly is crucial to the climax of *An American Dream* since it is his power that challenges Rojack to confront the disparate parts of himself. Yet, juxtaposed with the resourceful and dazzling performance of Martin, Kelly is incomplete. Martin poses in one role after another, as he enacts his scorn of Deborah, his familiarity with the public personality of Rojack, and his affair with Cherry. Yet at the same time, his mannered interpolations maintain the underlying presence of the hip black singer. Mailer is content to allow the irony and complexity of Martin's style to be demonstrated in the tone of his deliveries. His presence is enough to prove palpably his force as a catalyst in the growing love between Rojack and Cherry.

Similarly, the threat of inanimate waste that Rojack senses as he enters the Waldorf is powerfully dramatised by the incongrouous trio in Kelly's apartment. The grief over Deborah's sudden death, hypocritically shared between Bess, Eddie Ganucci and Kelly, thinly veils their inner moral corruption and physical decay. Like the apparent irrelevance of Martin's digressions, Bess's catlike attack on Ruta or Eddie Ganucci's story of his parrot illustrate the power of Mailer's satire when he maintains the economy of caricature. When, however, Kelly begins to relate the story of his rise to power, his relationship with Bess and incestuous desire for Deborah, he ceases to represent the mysterious convergence of legitimate and illegitimate power. As his virtually unbroken monologue progresses, he becomes Norman Mailer self-consciously offering credible illustrations to the claim that Kelly resides in Hell, that Bess is 'the most evil woman ever to live on the Riviera',(219) that Deborah was the worthy heiress of Kelly's corrupt legacy. The details of Kelly's account are fantastic but superfluous, because his calculated cunning has already been well established by the humorously oblique references to the network of his power. The presence of Eddie Ganucci, the representative of Mafia-wielded violence, conjoined with Kelly's casual mention of a phonecall from the White House expressing condolences, does more to consolidate his impressive control of institutionalised power than his assertion: ' "I decided the only explanation is that God and the Devil are very attentive to people at the summit . . . There's nothing but magic at the top" '.(248)

After the death of Cherry, Rojack escapes from the circumscribed world of his quest and sets out across America to Las Vegas. But just as New York represents Rojack's inner landscape, so the spaciousness of the continent is a mental topography. The cancerous patient, whose autopsy Rojack witnesses, is another example of the decay he senses in Eddie Ganucci. It is a sympton of the underlying madness which Rojack diagnoses as a national disease and which he knows that he himself embodies, so that Mailer shrouds the ultimate fate of his protagonist in deliberate ambiguity as he leaves Las Vegas 'something like sane again . . .'.(271) Mailer's determined effort to examine the implications of this ambiguity resulted in a series of brilliant achievements during the end of the 1960s.

3 'A Frustrated Actor'

Mailer's intimation that the profession of acting and that of writing may possess important analogies with regard to the form of his fictions, was first hinted at in 'Superman Comes to the Supermarket'. In this essay, Mailer was absorbed with the theory of acting rather that putting those theories into practise. In 1967 he ventured into the theatre with a dramatic adaptation of *The Deer Park*,[1] and produced, directed and performed in two films: *Wild 90* and *Beyond the Law*. In an essay occasioned by the filming of *Wild 90* called 'Some Dirt in the Talk', Mailer discusses his theories. A good actor, according to him, has an attachment to the reality before him, by pushing himself into styles of personality which are not quite himself but which will provide a more effective mode for handling events of the day. Like a good actor, the personae of Mailer's writing must be able to sift and select from the context of their acting in order to convey the truth of a situation. In 1971, Mailer's film *Maidstone*, which he had produced, directed and performed in four years earlier, was released. He also published an essay on this film in which he explains some of the difficulties of putting these theories into practice. Mailer realised that in evolving a persona whose style of acting would convey the reality—the truth—of a situation, 'It was as if there was a law that a person could not be himself in front of a camera unless he pretended to be someone other than himself'.[2] This dilemma is closely analogous to that which Mailer discovers in recounting his performance at the Ambassador Theatre in Washington. *The Armies of the Night* begins with the version reported in *Time*, which is principally concerned with Mailer's frequent obscenities. But in his own version of the event, Mailer is fascinated by his changing voices. He begins with a Southern accent, converts to a rhetoric that suggests 'Lincoln in hippieland',(57) till the use of the word 'shit' propels him forward to an aggressive tirade that mimics Cassius Clay, even while the voice proclaims he is 'Lyndon Johnson's little old *dwarf* alter ego'. At this point, 'Mailer thought quietly "My God, that is probably exactly

68

what you are at this moment, Lyndon Johnson with all his sores, sorrows, and vanity, squeezed down to five foot eight" '.(60) Part of Mailer's motive in giving this performance to the Ambassador's audience was his frustrated outrage at the political corruption that he felt contaminated the nation's leadership, which is obviously relieved by the savage parody. But, as he also stresses, his speech synthesised this 'external river' and an inner urge. There is 'the frustrated actor in Mailer—ever since seeing *All the King's Men* years ago, he had wanted to come on in public as a Southern demagogue'.(62)

The ideas that are suggested by this kind of performance also have a direct relevence to the form of *Why Are We in Vietnam?* The development of Mailer's first-person narrators, from Sergius O'Shaugnessy in 'The Time of Her Time', to D.J. in *Why Are We in Vietnam?* lies in the fact that they are not distinguished as consistent, physically-cut human types. They maintain their presence in the story or novel through a style of voice which presents a deliberately problematical physical embodiment. Mailer explained this notion to Steven Marcus in the *Paris Review* interview given in 1967. Replying to Marcus' question, ' "Can you describe how you turn a real person into a fictional one?" ', he explained how a character separates from the model who inspired it.

> It's when they become almost as complex as one's own personality that the fine excitement begins. Because then they are not really characters any longer—they're beings, which is a distinction I like to make. A character is someone you can grasp as a whole, you can have a clear idea of him, but a being is someone whose nature keeps shifting.(248)

D. J. is complex like Mailer's own personality; he is a series of rapidly shifting voices; he performs like Mailer. As a conventional character, however, he possesses as much substantiality as the brief appearance of 'L. B. J.' on the stage of the Ambassador Theatre, while his voice functions, like the voice of 'L. B. J.' as a simultaneous outlet for his creator's political disgust and exhuberant exhibitionist delight.

Mailer had been reaching toward this notion of the omnipresent narrative voice as early as his concluding piece to *Advertisements for Myself*: 'Advertisements For Myself On The Way Out'. After an awkward preamble in which the narrator coyly speculates, 'am I ghost, embryo, intellect, wind of the unconscious, or some part of

Him or Her or Hem or Hir?', he goes on to include, as possible
embodiments for his voice, an old house, a tree, a flower, the ocean
and sand dunes, and finally a dog.(424–5) In a determined effort to
compound his lack of substance, he finally insists upon utilising the
insubstantiality of the wind 'because I now feel the frustration of a
wind which knows so much and can tell your ears so little'.(430)
Besides the fact that these possible physical correlatives, with the
exception of the wind, are listed with a seemingly casual arbitrari-
ness, the narrative appears perversely confusing because the
omnipresent narrator exists on a conceptual level only. There is
nothing to corroborate this theme in the language used.

While *Deaths For The Ladies (and other disasters)*, published three
years later in 1962, was critically assessed as yet another quirky
adventure of Mailer, this volume of poems, quite apart from
possessing some intrinsic merit, served as an opportunity for Mailer
to develop his controlling facility with varieties of verbal and
literary styles. Echoes of popular song, Wallace Stevens, T. S. Eliot,
e. e. cummings for example, are juxtaposed with seemingly self-
conscious whimsy that on closer examination, demonstrates a
resourceful and humorous awareness of the performing voice:

>   Colored people
>   have beautiful
>   hands
>   said the pause

>   Listen
>   mother
>   fucker
>   said
>   the mood
>   Stop quoting me.[3]

In his introduction to this volume, Mailer called it 'a movie in
words', stressing the importance of the placing of the word on the
page and the significance of repeating certain phrases 'like images in
a film'. The cinematic analogy that Mailer uses to describe his 'most
modern poem about a man loose in our city' bears a singular

resemblance to the manner in which the voices of D. J. are manipulated in *Why Are We in Vietnam?* It also prefigures Mailer's discussion on the role of the camera eye in his essay published with the script of his film *Maidstone*. Mailer makes a distinction between the use and abuse of the film camera. It can be used, he argues, to suggest the ambiguity of the actors it focuses upon, so that although they are caught in the plot, they do not belong to it altogether. The camera therefore calls attention to its technique, which invests a large degree of uncertainty in the extent to which a person, situation or emotion really exists or is being invented. The camera though can also be reduced to the anonymity of the mass-media. D. J.'s voice has a similar dual function in compounding the mystery of his consciousness, which places the existence of his character in a problematic light, whilst simultaneously endorsing and duplicating the instant vacuity of the popular media.

Although the form of the narrative, to which D. J. constantly draws attention, is subject to the selectivity of his memory, Mailer does not intend his point of view to be mistrusted both in the interpretation as well as the reporting of events. He became deeply absorbed in the possibilities of eradicating script, encouraging the blurring of the boundary between acted and sincerely felt emotion, using the hand-held camera as if it were an extension of the eye, and, most important, the enormous repercussions of film editing. It therefore became obvious to Mailer that the uncertainty of each event, each statement, was a positive provocation to the audience: 'It expanded one's notion of cinematic possibilities, and it intensified one's awareness of the moment. When significant movement was captured, it was now doubly significant because one could not take it for granted'.(163) The theory of context, stressing the importance of previous and related moments, was now given a new emphasis. With the notion of withdrawing personally from this kind of creative process and insisting upon its mechanistic procedure, Mailer capitalised on the mystery and the ambiguity of this kind of form. This is exactly what he intends by describing the uncertainty of D. J.'s memory and powers of interpretation. He is duplicating, in D. J.'s shifting point of view, the confusion of dream, the underground river of the pysche as Mailer puts it, where we, the reader, are never certain how far we can trust D. J., how far we can believe in a statement after it has been cleared from the surrounding verbiage. So the unfolding of his narrative is, like the unrolling of a film, part of the mechanism of memory, or at least, a most peculiar annex to memory. For in film we remember events as if they had taken place and we were there. But we were not. The psyche has taken into itself a whole country of fantasy and made it psychologically real, made it a part of memory.(149–50)

The importance of cutting a film, primarily with a view to disturbing the viewer at a subconscious level, rather than to further the continuity of the story, is practised by Mailer in the montage of D.J.'s voice. Far from simply duplicating confusion and discord in the form of the narrative, he was also discovering a decided syntax in the seemingly arbitrary jump of one 'frame' to the next.

D.J.'s most conventional embodiment (in fictional terms) is that of Ranald Jethroe Jellicoe Jethroe who is the son of Alice Hallie Lee Jethroe and Rutherford David Jethroe Jellicoe Jethroe (Rusty for short). Rusty is a director of '4C and P',[4] the manufacturers of a plastic filter for cigarettes which also causes cancer of the lip. The narrative of the novel describes the penetration of a group of Texan Corporation Executives, headed by Rusty, into Alaska in order to hunt for big game. They are accompanied by Ranald and his blood brother, Tex Hyde. The guide for the trip is Luke Fellinka of the Moe Henry and Obungekat Safari Group who takes them on a trip into Brooks Range, north of the Arctic Circle. The pattern of this trip, from urban and industrialised Texas to primitive Alaska obviously draws upon a major theme of American literature, from Mark Twain to William Faulkner. But the primitive north has been infected by the technological corruption of Rusty and his counterparts, giving the theme a contemporary relevance. Hunting is conducted from helicopters, the hunters rely upon the destructive machinery of their armoury rather than upon their own skills, and even Luke, the guide, has cynically succumbed: 'he was an American, what the fuck, he had spent his life living up tight with wilderness and that had eaten at him, wilderness was tasty but boredom was his corruption, he had wanted a jolt . . . Big Luke now got his kicks with the helicopter'.(68) Luke aids and abets the destruction of the animals he had once known and understood: 'Cop Turds are exploding psychic ecology all over the place . . .'.(79) The animals, especially bears, are insane; they attack and kill with no provocation.

The virtues of equal combat have been destroyed by people like Rusty. Instead of war being a balanced confrontation between two opposing sides with an unknown outcome, it has become a totalitarian attack with a view to annihilation. Rusty explains:

> I like the feeling that if I miss a vital area I still can count on the big impact knocking them down, killing them by the total impact, shock! It's like aerial bombardment in the last Big War . . . It's just like if you get in a fight with a fellow, you're well advised to destroy him half to death. If y'get him down, use your shoe on his face, employ your imagination, give him a working-over . . . .(59)

Since Rusty believes that brutality should accompany a one-to-one combat as well as a massed impersonal national force, he is a Cannibal, according to Mailer's definition in his introduction to *Cannibals and Christians*: he will 'kill and . . . eliminate' which 'is his sense of human continuation'.(18) In hunting bear, not only is Rusty's personal reputation in 4C and P at stake, but the reputation of America, and, by implication, the world: ' . . . he reads the world's doom in his own fuckup. If he is less great than God intended him to be, then America is in Trouble.'(77) It is irrelevant how the bear is hunted and killed. If there is some heroism in Rusty taking off alone with Ranald and hunting without the aid of Luke's machinery, it is forced upon him by Luke's fear of endangering his clients' lives. It does not stop him from bombarding a dying bear with unnecessary bullets. After the bear's violent death, 'legs thrashing, brain exploding from new galvanizings and overloadings of massive damage report . . .', (101) Rusty claims the carcase as his own trophy. D. J. cannot forgive his father for cutting short a communion that he is enjoying with the peace in the eyes of the dying bear, and simply remarks after Rusty's claim, 'Whew. Final end of love of one son for one father.'(ibid)

D. J., alias Ranald, makes an attempt to break free of the 'specific mix of mixed old shit'(140) by journeying above the snowline into Brooks Range with Tex Hyde. They jettison their weapons and experience the fear and exhilaration of equal combat with their environment. The white wolf is repulsed by the waves of animal aggression from the two boys: 'Two waves of murder, human and animal, meet across the snow in a charge as fantastic and beautiful as Alexander Nevsky . . .'.(125) A world of which D. J. and Tex were completely unaware is revealed, where the outwitting of Fox by Squirrel provides a humorous entertainment that is balanced by the beauty of the Arctic meadows. The boys begin to realise, however, that the cruel destruction and consumption of flesh is not reserved to the hunters. They watch from a tree as a bear kills a caribou calf, and becomes bored and disgusted with more flesh than he can eat. D. J. remembers the bear that Rusty finally killed, into whose dying eyes D. J. gazed and which seemed 'to be drawing in the peace of the forest preserved for all animals as they die, the unspoken cool on tap in the veins of every tree . . .'.(101) This peace is notably absent from 'Griz # 2' and D. J. experiences intense curiosity in wondering whether this bear would die like 'Griz # 1 as if the center of all significant knowledge right there'.(133) This dilemma presents itself to D. J. when the eyes of the first kill of the hunt—a wolf by Tex Hyde—are examined. Is the true nature of 'Signor Lupo' contained in the eye which 'had the pain of the madman who knows there's a better world but he is excluded' or in the eye 'full of sunlight and peace, a harvest sun on late afternoon field . . . ?'(50)

At least D. J. comes to develop a sympathy with nature such that he is willing to admit that the question of the cruelty and madness of the wilderness versus its beauty and peace is a crucially significant one. When he earlier examines the eyes of 'Signor Lupo' he cuts off his reflection with 'shit! It was just an animal eye like the glass they use for an eye in a trophy . . .'.(ibid) He is content to use Luke's helicopter, along with the rest of the company, although by this time aware of the shame of this style of hunting.' . . . he was only part of them [the animals], and part he was of gasoline of Texas, the asshole sulfur smell of money-oil clinging to the helicopter . . .'.(69)

There is no conclusive answer to the problem as it is posed by D. J. alias Ranald. The true nature of the wilderness remains an enigma. For D. J. and Tex, alone under the Arctic lights, God reveals himself as a beast, whose directive is ' "Go out and kill—fulfill my will, go and kill" '.(140) They return as killer brothers to the 'same specific mix of mixed old shit'(ibid) fully equipped to fight in the Vietnam war. There could be no other resolution to their venture because both have been conditioned to be killers. D. J. when five years old was attacked by Rusty in a football tackle and saw the desire to murder in his father's eyes. Tex is the son of an undertaker and has inherited the nature of a killer. They are both a 'peculiar blendaroon of humanity and evil, technological know how, pure savagery, sweet aching secret American youth, and sheer downright meanness. . .'.(112)

The American wilderness has always provided a convenient metaphor for the nature of man when he is confronted and challenged by its power. *Why Are We in Vietnam?* is no exception in that the savagery which confronts Tex and D. J. is an accurate reflection, not a cause, of that brutal aspect of the American character. The cause of this killer instinct in enacted in the electronic performance of D. J.'s voice, the confusion of whose brain 'might be a tape recording, right?'(18) but who is simultaneously 'a genius', the 'only American alive who could outtalk Cassius Clay . . .'.(17) In the first Intro Beep, D. J. repeatedly stresses that 'There is probably no such thing as a totally false perception'(7) and then presents the possibility that the medium for this infinite objectivity is 'a tape recorded in heaven . . .'.(8) Intro Beep 2 however undermines the notion that this consciousness which could be 'put down *forever* on a tiny piece of microfilm'(19) is, despite its extraordinary gymnastics, reliable. D. J.'s voice introduces an uncertain variant into his electronic medium which directly contradicts his assurance in the opening Intro Beep. D. J. 'may be trying to trick Number One Above, maybe I'm putting false material into *this* tape recorder, or jamming it—contemplate!'(19–20) With this contradiction, D. J. immediately introduces the problematic nature of his voice. Is he endorsing the McLuhanite premise that the medium is indeed the message—or is he, by means of his belligerent evasiveness, counteracting the denial of selfhood that McLuhan's thesis would seem to advance?

Mailer is using D. J.'s voice for both purposes. On the one hand, D. J. is an admirer of McLuhan. He performs, with brilliant facility, the lightning-like verbal shifts from relevancy to irrelevancy purely in order to demonstrate the speed of his mental connections, and smugly pronounces that 'Old McLuhan's going to be breaking his fingernails all over again when he hears this'.(18) What D. J. is presenting in his role as a McLuhanite disc jockey is reserved for Intro Beep 10, by which time D. J. alias Ranald and Tex are journeying alone into the foothills of Brooks Range. The electronic medium which is D. J.'s voice is referred to here as 'the undiscovered magnetic-electro fief of the dream',(116) convertible into light waves and termed the Universal Mind. D. J. exhuberantly elaborates upon his terminology and reveals that he is describing no less than the subconscious of America. Each person is thus reduced to being a component of 'the dream fief' which is received by 'that land above the Circle . . .'.(118)

Mailer is parodying the extreme optimism and determinism of McLuhan in this manifestation of D. J.'s voice. Like McLuhan, D. J. sees the selfhood of man as being wholly determined by outside circumstances. In *Understanding Media*, McLuhan's discussion of 'Media as Translators' serves as a footnote to D. J.'s explication of man's 'MEF trip ticket':(117)

> In this electric age we see ourselves being translated more and more into the form of information, moving toward the technological extension of consciousness. That is what is meant when we say that we daily know more and more about man. We mean that we can translate more and more of ourselves into other forms of expression that exceed ourselves . . .
>
> By putting our physical bodies inside our extended nervous systems, by means of electric media, we set up a dynamic by which all previous technologies that are mere extensions of hands and feet and teeth and bodily heat-controls—all such extensions of our bodies, including cities—will be translated into information systems. Electromagnetic technology requires utter human docility and quiescence of meditation such as benefits an organism that now wears its brain outside its skull and its nerves outside its hide.[5]

As Rusty, his Medium Ass-holes Pete and Bill, D. J. alias Ranald and Tex Hyde confront the wilderness of Alaska, D. J. demonstrates how man's inner control of each of his senses has been corrupted by the external manipulation exerted by electromagnetic technology. If, as McLuhan claims, 'it is now possible to program ratios among the senses that approach the condition of consciousness',[6] man is unable to cope with or understand a simple and direct stimulus to one of his senses. D. J. chooses the sense of smell on which to concentrate and describes his feeling of excited unease during his first night under canvas. The North has 'a tricky clean smell, like a fine nerve washed in alcohol . . .'.(48) He imagines Rusty thinking of bear and fearfully smelling pine around the bunkhouse, which 'smells like no pine forest Rusty ever saw, for the odor goes in and in again until he is afraid to breathe all the way, aisles are opening in his brain before the incense of it which is like the odor of the long fall in a dream'.(74–5) In jettisoning their guns and moving above the snowline toward the Arctic, D. J. and Tex finally learn that they have been so conditioned by the electronic manipulation of their

senses, that it is terrifying to move purely 'on smell'.(126) It is a
conditioning that cannot be undone; and it is not just the hunters
whose selfhood has been electronically truncated but the animals
too. There is madness in the air which DJ beams into and relays
back for our edification. The bear who sends out his message, 'don't
come near, motherfuck'(39) is subject to a system that has corrupted
the very substance of the wilderness by reducing it to a mass message
'that Alaska air is the real message—it says don't bullshit,
buster'.(ibid) There is no leavening to the hopelessness that this
manifestation of D. J. outlines. His determinism appears all the
more disturbing in its frantically optimistic presentation. It is
illuminating to juxtapose this McLuhanite parody with Mailer's
own views on the media, which have become increasingly pessimistic. In 1962, in 'An Impolite Interview', he argued with Paul
Krassner that the mass-media were a cause of the totalitarian
mediocrity of America because they were controlled by people who
wanted power for the sake of it. Mailer believes this will lead
towards Fascism 'because it [a bad television show] is meretricious
art and so sickens people a little further'.(147) He specified this
statement when he went on to condemn the art of the absurd, in
Cannibals and Christians, which bases its form on disconnection, on
irreconcilable images. In *The Armies of the Night*, Mailer argues that,
like D. J.'s voice, the media, especially television, are similar to
absurd art in that the minds who receive its impulses are:

> jabbed and poked and twitched and probed and finally galva-
> nized into surrealistic modes of response by commercials cutting
> into dramatic narratives . . . forced willy-nilly to build their idea
> of the space–time continuum (and therefore their nervous
> system) on the jumps and cracks and leaps and breaks which
> every phenomenon from the media seemed to contain within
> it.(98)

Mailer's most savage attack upon the cause of mass mediocrity is
found in *St George and the Godfather* (1972) where he could focus his
outrage upon a single figure—Richard Nixon—a patent product
and personification of the media. Because, according to Mailer, the
Republicans had controlled and arranged their Convention so that
it was orchestrated like a bad television show, the only reaction
allowed to media men and protesting youth alike was to treat the
communication itself as the Convention. The totalitarianism that

Mailer discerns in the influence of the media is nowhere more apparent than in the development from his description of the radical youth, caught by his prose in frozen attitudes of Bosch-like impotence, unable to protest effectively at all:

> across the screens of the nation they flurry, cawing like gulls in adenoidal complaints, a medieval people's band of lepers and jesters who put a whiff of demonology on the screen, or lay an entertaining shiver along the incantations of their witches. Did that hint of a gay demented air now serve only to dignify the battlements of the white knights of Christendom up on Nixon Heights?[7]

These startling images define a familiar opposition, albeit an ironic one. With the protestors as demonic witches arrayed against Nixon as the Christian white knight, it is no longer possible to understand the terms of the conflict, let alone envisage the two meeting in any meaningful confrontation. When opposing forces are frozen into incoherencies or contradictions, then the warring encounter is, like Rusty's shoe in the face, an 'aerial bombardment'.(59)

Nevertheless, there is in D. J.'s voice a manifest presence that attempts to sabotage the frozen polarity between the hunters and the hunted. This presence presents itself as a mystery that even he does not necessarily comprehend. He admits that the conversation between his mother and Dr Rothenberg, or the reveries of Rusty, are inventions of his own. He throws into extreme doubt the independent existence of all the characters in the narrative. They are clearly representatives of easily recognisable types; beyond that, there are no means by which their individuality can be corroborated. In undermining the objective validity of his narrative, D. J. is not weakening his own position of authority. He introduces a set of opposing embodiments for his voice to act as a corrective to the sterility of the 'riptide impact and collision area marginated halfway between civilization and a nature culture—primitive constellation (like Alaska, man) . . .'.(64) On three occasions, he introduces the possibility that he is a 'Spade and writing like a Shade . . . pretending to write a white man's fink fuck book in revenge . . .'.(20) Yet each time the possibility is introduced, D. J. takes a delight in complicating this duality of consciousness by questioning who is imagining whom.

The dual consciousness of D. J. is a culmination of Mailer's thesis first developed in 'The White Negro', but it is apparent that Mailer is also mocking his own thesis. It exists as a convenient, almost clichéd opposition, like the other *döppelganger* that D. J. presents for our confusion. He is Dr Jekyll in more than one exhuberant tirade and the significance of this appellation is made apparent when his blood brother, Tex Hyde, is introduced. Although Tex exists as Rusty, Luke, Medium Ass-holes Pete and Bill exist, as a part of the narrative, his existence, like the Harlem spade, could also be a capricious and playful whim on the part of D. J. It is nevertheless important that these problematic oppositions inhabit D. J.'s consciousness. They demonstrate that there is no corrective to the incoherent contradictions that D. J. as disc jockey has picked up in the air and defined as animal madness and national sickness.

The partnership of D. J. alias Dr. Jekyll and Tex Hyde culminates in a sexual confrontation which both are afraid to act upon since they are caught in a 'conflict of lust to own the other yet in fear of being killed by the other . . .'.(140) Both Rusty Jethroe and Gottfried Hyde have used sex decreatively as a means to exert power for its own sake. Rusty surrounds himself with Ass-holes who sycophantically endorse his status; Gottfried sexually ravages anything that presents itself as a physical possibility. D. J. and Tex have inherited this sexual opportunism; their attitude to women is crude and casual and their temptation to commit buggery is not only inherently decreative, but converts them into 'killer brothers . . .'.

The event is a climactic confrontation that emerges from a system of sexual metaphors that D. J.'s voice employs in order to stress the destructive clash between civilisation and the wilderness. He functions like the crystal which he defines as 'a receiving apparatus to draw in messages, because it's a form, man, a crystal is the most acute kind of form and forms are receptors of that which is less formed because that which is less formed looks to define itself by getting fucked by a form'.(105) D. J.'s voice then is like the 'icy wilderness',(118) rigidified, a frustrated impulse which can only attain a fluidity by being creatively 'fucked'. The assault of the hunters' guns, exhaustively classified in Chapter Five, upon the 'beautiful castrating cunt' of mother nature(126) metaphorically enacts the failure of D. J.'s crystal receiving voice to be fertilised by the form of his narrative.

D. J. maintains a dense analogy between sexual impotence and sexual abuse and the hunting procedures of his characters in order to demonstrate the immensity of loss in the solitude of Brooks Range. He imagines Rusty's sense of dread the night before his first opportunity to shoot bear and while holding off the urge to masturbate, compares his own and Rusty's anticipation to the client who was reduced to impotence with a Saskatchewan whore because 'he was afraid he would blast himself if he ever blew it into her . . . '. (79) The guns of the hunters are just such impotent phalluses when they maim and reduce to madness the animals they pursue. When D. J. and Rusty are alone, and enjoying temporary and uneasy intimacy with the woods, the prospect of bear quarry is compared to the excitement of sexual fulfilment, but it remains dehumanised, juvenile, uncontrolled. The only method by which the wilderness can be sensed in its terrifying beauty which maintains some freedom from the 'mixed shit' that threatens it, is to remain 'unfucked'. Even as D. J. insists upon this truth, corroborating it with a description of the heaven of seeing Dall ram, Fox, Squirrel, Griz and the Arctic meadow covered with beautiful flowers, his language retains its obscene brutality. Despite the sensitivity in D. J.'s voice to the necessity of a maintained polarity between mother nature and the guns (the shit is, after all, a result of mixing), his language compulsively enacts the frustrated impulse of the rigid form reaching for some kind of creative release.

Yet set against this there is the description of the sunset and the moose when D. J. alias Ranald and Tex Hyde spend their only night alone in the wilderness of Brooks Range. While refusing to allow awe to eliminate the 'knobby knees and dumb red little eyes' (136) of the moose, which is consistent with D. J.'s disclaimer on the eyes of the wolf, he goes on to eulogise the grandeur of the animal within the context of the landscape and rising moon. The continuity of the prose culminating in an unexpected beauty and seriousness of sentiment immediately achieves an effect that Mailer, in his essay on Maidstone, describes as 'the *déjà vu*' (167) of skilful film cutting. The confused attitude of D. J. in his previous encounters with dead and dying animals is now seen as a genuine ambiguity expressing the dilemma of the impact and collision of the so-called civilised and the primitive.

The problematic identity of not only D. J. but also Stephen Rojack illustrates an important notion that Mailer attempts to explain in his interview with Steven Marcus in the *Paris Review* (reprinted in *Cannibals and Christians*). In response to Marcus' question, ' "Would you say something about style, prose style, in relation to the novel?" ', Mailer explains,

> 'A really good style comes only when a man has become as good as he can be. Style is character. A good style cannot come from a bad undisciplined character. Now a man may be evil, but I believe that people can be evil in their essential natures and still have good characters. Good in the sense of being well tuned. They can have characters which are flexible, supple, adaptable, principled in relation to their own good or their own evil . . . '.(246)

Mailer is using 'good' in two senses here, although he does not, in this context, make it clear. Characters can be principled in relation to their own evil as well as their own good if they are 'well tuned' into their fictional context. Mailer is refering here to a process whereby the formal skills of the writer control and ultimately transform these moral polarities within his characters into a meaningful dialectic. It is by means of these criteria that Rojack's murder of Deborah and his courtship of Cherry might be assessed, or D. J. alias Ranald's simultaneous contempt and awe for the wilderness. But in Mailer's response to Marcus' question, there is also an indication of the development in his writing from *An American Dream* and *Why Are We in Vietnam?* to *The Armies of the Night*. Marcus quite specifically refers to the prose style of the novelist. Yet Mailer's answer makes no distinction between the writer and his character, so that he concludes with a reflection upon a style that has clearly departed from Marcus' sense of the word— ' "Writers who are possessed of some physical grace may tend to write better than writers who are physically clumsy" '.(246) It is this concept of style that shapes the personae of Mailer's protagonists in *The Armies of the Night* and *Maidstone*, who are generally divided upon the distinction between actor and spectator.

When Mailer cautiously committed himself to the anti-Vietnam march in Washington, which took place in October 1967, a combination of determination, courage and fortunate circumstance placed him at the centre of events which culminated in a demonstration outside the Pentagon. Mailer deliberately provoked the police to arrest him by crossing a Military Police Line. For the first time, events which held moral implications that were both personally and nationally momentous, enabled Mailer to create a protagonist whose autonomy was unquestioned. The authority of the protagonist's speculations and judgements is endorsed by personal drama which is both distinct from and yet part of a collective political context. The cultural and fictional realms which the protagonist of *The Armies of the Night* inhabits prompted Mailer to focus his subsequent writing and other activities upon the problematic relationship between these two realms and relinquish entirely the form of self-contained fiction.[8]

The success of Mailer's achievements in this often ambiguous genre is, however, a vexed question. An illustration of this critical difficulty is provided in the persistent preoccupation of Mailer's protagonists with the notion of the Presidency. In constantly hovering over the image of national leadership, it is hard to discern, at this point in Mailer's career, where he is attempting to define a national malaise and its possible antidote, and where he is merely giving voice to a long-indulged but repressed fantasy. It is more than likely that Mailer was practically exploring the apparent anomaly of the individual and institutionalised mind that he discerned in John Kennedy. In 'An Imaginary Interview', published in 1967, Mailer used the form of an internal dialogue, similar to that of 'The Metaphysics of the Belly' and 'The Political Economy of Time' to stress wryly both the arrogance and modesty of his ambitions:

> Mailer: . . . I am not afraid of questions. A man who can't answer questions shouldn't run for President.
> Interviewer: Are you really still running?
> Mailer: Only for President of the literary world.
> Interviewer: Well, even there you've got a way to go. There's opposition, Mr Mailer, considerable opposition.
> Mailer: Still, I think I'm the best candidate around. It's a modest remark, believe me, because the best isn't necessarily that good. At any rate, I'm prepared to wait for office. (217)

Writing in *The Armies of the Night* of the March which took place the month following the publication of this 'interview', Mailer's simultaneous desire to be arrested and to attend a party in New York provokes the reflection: 'Yes, Mailer had an egotism of curious disproportions. With the possible exception of John F. Kennedy, there had not been a President of the United States, nor even a candidate since the Second World War whom Mailer secretly considered more suitable than himself . . .'.(131) As yet, the notion of Presidential office serves as a useful image to stress the political, cultural and social responsibilities that the protagonist of *The Armies of the Night* is prepared to assume in his fictional form. In the summer of 1968, however, Mailer played the role of a film director who was also running for President. It was, of course, an election year; Mailer had attended and written about both Conventions and had been in Chicago when Bobby Kennedy was assassinated in San Francisco. To choose to centre a film around the possible assassination of a Presidential candidate was therefore both important and topical. Yet in *Maidstone*, where Mailer deliberately obfuscates the distinguishing criteria between reality and acting, the Presidency is not only the ambition of Norman T. Kingsley but also serves to illustrate the unchallenged power that both the real and acted film director exerts over his cast and camera crew.

In both *The Armies of the Night* and *Maidstone*, however, the Presidential figure is successfully used to point out how the artist in his several roles is able to expose the inner contradictions of the national leader, by acting the role himself. In his essay on *Maidstone*, Mailer points out:

> . . . if I was trying to do one single thing in this movie, I was trying to show a man who runs for President—well, look at the incredible contradictory qualities such a man has to have. Now of course, the man I had running for President could never in reality run, but in fantasy he could, and in fantasy he could be a parallel to a man like, anyone, like Nixon, Rockefeller, Humphrey, even McCarthy.(116)

Mailer was not content, however, to channel his notions of the exercise of political leadership into his writing, directing and acting. In the summer of 1969, he was a candidate for the mayoralty of New York with Jimmy Breslin as his running mate. The ticket on which he ran, proposing that New York City be made the fifty-first state, was brilliant, well-argued and demonstrated the extent to which Mailer understood the economic and social crisis which the city faced. Yet his campaigning style exposed a confusion of the roles of writer and politician; his style as a politician was too often compromised by his instinctive desire to be Norman Mailer the writer acting the role of a politician. When Mailer proposed to run for mayor of New York in 1960, James Baldwin protested: 'I do not feel that a writer's responsibility can be discharged in this way. I do not think, if one is a writer, that one escapes it by trying to become something else. One does not become something else: one becomes nothing'.[9] Mailer was not trying to be something else; he was carrying to its logical extreme the conviction that had remained with him ever since the publication of *Advertisements for Myself*—that his soul symbolised the nation's soul. Presenting himself to the public as a candidate for political office was a natural extension of the opening declaration of *Advertisements for Myself*: 'I have been running for President these last ten years in the privacy of my mind . . .'.(17) But Baldwin is right in the sense that Mailer the candidate is not a protagonist whose activities are a context that can subsequently become the form which the artist constructs to demonstrate that 'politics are an extension of personal lives'.[10] Joe Flaherty, Mailer's campaign manager, became understandably exasperated as he noticed that Mailer's reaction to adverse press articles was as a writer and not as a politician, that he was unable to master the little touches of the campaigner and relied instead on the magnetism of his name and reputation.

In other words, Mailer is not making the necessary distinction between the procedures and truths of politics and the procedures and truths of art. In discussing the relationship between literature and society, George Panichas makes a point that illuminates the confusion that Mailer's ambition fell prey to during the year that separates his most recent venture into film-making from his mayoral campaign. 'The subject of literature and society can be of value if the criteria of interpretation do not in themselves become political-ized . . .',[11] and he goes on to emphasise the importance of 'the need to be aware of the full power of the ideological forces that constitute the social–political vision, and of the way in which dialectical elements affect a writer's vision'.[12] Mailer was in full possession of this awareness when he wrote *The Armies of the Night*, but it is relevant to consider some of the pressures that were strong enough to propel him towards the arena of practical politics first in 1960 and again in 1969, despite the disaster of that first attempt. The central image of *The Armies of the Night* is the Pentagon, which symbolises that national malaise that Mailer labels totalitarianism. 'High church of the corporation, the Pentagon spoke exclusively of mass man and his civilization; every aspect of the building was anonymous, monotonous, interchangeable'.(240–1) The obvious antidote to this 'monotonous' and 'massive' power that wields its pernicious influence on every aspect of national life is the revolutionary overthrow of the American superstate. Yet the notion of a successful revolutionary change is only tolerable to the novelist's imagination. The Left proliferate out of 'alphabet soups'(106) of labels whose abstractions are unwittingly the dupes of 'technology land . . .'.(107) 'Mailer detested it, cursed those logics of commitment which carried him into such formal lines of protest'.(66) His distaste springs from a conviction that 'Existentially, it hardly mattered whether the logic came from a Communist, Trotskyist, Splinter Marxist, union organizer, or plain Social Democrat'.(96) In a bureaucratic superstate, the ideology that precedes a revolution makes it no revolution at all. The alternative lies in the New Left who, taking their cue from Cuba, embark on a political action whose revolutionary end is unknown. Yet Mailer feels a sense of frustration in that this attack is forced to be a symbolic manoeuvre by the nature of its enemy. The Pentagon is immune to actual invasion because its control is decentralised. The most the New Left can hope for is to inspire authority with horror and bewilderment, being unable to understand 'a movement which inspired thousands and hundreds of thousands to march without a coordinated plan'.(99) Mailer's own revolution is found in the 'apocalyptic garden'(106) of 'a gun in the hills'(89) which he admits he formerly thought of as a game 'where finally you never got hurt if you played the game well enough'.(ibid) Disillusionment comes to Mailer with the characteristic realisation that he is too much of a figurehead for this anonymous form of warfare and must therefore be prepared to be victimised as a political prisoner of the future. Being arrested and imprisoned for twenty-four hours temporarily assuages that foreboding, as well as providing the brilliant climax of *The Armies of the Night*. It was the chafing conviction that a radical change must be effected, however, along with the belief that all existing revolutionary and Left-wing ideologies and groups were exhausted, that propelled Mailer into the political arena as a one-man show, or, in his own terminology, as a Left-conservative.

Mailer is discussed, along with Dwight Macdonald, by Christopher Lasch in his examination of the American radical of the 1940s, 1950s and 1960s. The radical's dilemma, according to Lasch, is that although revolution from the 1950s on never seemed more appropriate, it remained remote because of the incalculable power of the nation-state. The situation worsened with the realisation that, despite the fact that the Cold War gave the appearance that East versus West offered an ideological choice, there was little to choose between them as superstates. The radical, Lasch argues, has reached the end of ideology and 'The fact is that politics without ideology, whatever else it may be, tends to become somewhat boring; and it was necessary for most people to put the ideology back into politics, whether it belonged there or not'.[13] In his attempt to regain 'the old blend of culture and politics'[14] Mailer was promoting his own peculiar ideology which rejected neither the Left nor the Right, but skirted the intolerable aspects of both, as a practical alternative to 'the apocalyptic garden'(106) of his revolution, which belonged too exclusively to the fictionalist. In the event, his mayoral campaign proved that the political candidate was heir to the White Negro and the protagonist of 'Superman Comes to the Supermarket'.

In *The Armies of the Night*, however, Mailer exercised a control over his several roles in a literary form that marked the height of his achievement in fictional journalism. In this book, Mailer solves the problem of maintaining a direct connection between the perceptions and opinions of his protagonist and the issues and events that provoke them by making him the principal public participant. There is no public luminary that can arguably outshine the figure of Norman Mailer at the March. Because David Dellinger and Jerry Rubin organised the event, they can resolve nothing of its central ambiguity: their roles are too inflexibly partisan. Mailer, however, states the requirements of a point of view that can resolve this ambiguous event:

> he must be not only involved, but ambiguous in his own proportions, a comic hero, which is to say, one cannot happily resolve the emphasis of the category—is he finally comic, a ludicrous figure with mock-heroic associations; or is he not unheroic, and therefore embedded somewhat tragically in the comic? Or is he both at once, and all at once?(64)

Mailer manages to fulfil this grand promise of versatility because the form of his narrative rests not only upon the activity of the protagonist but also upon the problematic relationship between the protagonist and his creator and the media's several versions of that uneasy relationship. In *The Armies of the Night*, therefore, Mailer has solved his earlier problem of establishing a clear distinction between himself and his protagonist by making it one of the themes of his book.

On three distinct occasions the several personae are abandoned in favour of Mailer, who reflects upon the difficulties of the private man coping with the various versions of his public legend. Torn between a dual loyalty to act out or write about his protest against the Vietnamese war, Mailer realises that he must first commit himself to the former, since he had as a writer 'been suffering more and more in the past few years from the private conviction that he was getting a little soft, a hint curdled, perhaps an almost invisible rim of corruption was growing around the edges. His career, his legend, his idea of himself—were they stale?'(69) After being arrested, Mailer ponders upon the possibility of provoking a second arrest and reaches the decision not to on the basis of the media's adverse reaction: '(Mailer's habit of living—no matter how unsuccessfully—with his image, was so engrained by now, that like a dutiful spouse he was forever consulting his better half)'.(173) When the protagonist, in the role of spouse, discusses his 'quintessentially American'(183) wife, he embarks on a discussion whose subject is both an image for the purpose of the protagonist's argument and a literal reality for the creator of that protagonist. To Mailer, his marriage reflects his 'love affair with America',(182) since the emotions that both wife and country evoke are 'damnably parallel . . .'.(ibid) Mailer and the protagonist of *The Armies of the Night* jostle one another in the drama of the argument in their effort to lay claim to their respective versions of this woman.

> Forget all pride as a husband, a lover, a man—the novelist in him was outraged. To live four years with a woman and not be able to decide if her final nature was good or evil? That might make for great interest in a marriage, much trickiness to love, large demands for manly discipline, but what was the novelist to think of himself?—especially when he (like all novelists) prided himself on his knowledge of women.(ibid)

While Mailer supplements the roles of his protagonist with mock heroic versions of his own, the interpretation that the press offers of his activities undermines them through distortion. By ending Book One as he began, with a distorted press account of the protagonist's speech-making, he demonstrates that the press, like all mass-media, do not report an event: their report is the event. The speech at the Ambassador Theatre, drunkenly peppered with obscenities, is diametrically opposed in mood and sentiment to the Christian speech outside Occoquan. Yet the style of both *Time* and *The Washington Post* is patronising, wryly tolerant and, of course, inaccurate. The *Time* report, however, also serves a fictional purpose. By presenting an obviously inadequate account of a series of bizarre and violent events, Mailer immediately creates an anticipatory suspense that can then be controlled by the narrative's point of view.

The several personae that compose the protagonist of *The Armies of the Night*, however, are the authoritative base on which the form of the narrative rests. Part One begins with Mitch Goodman persuading Mailer to add his name to the list of notables who will join the anti-Vietnam March, and ends with the first climax which is the débâcle at the Washington Theatre. The inception of the March is peripheral in Book One since the protagonist is primarily the participant who modestly qualifies as an eyewitness of the events. Mailer is able to imbue his narrative with mounting drama since he has created a participant who is at first bored by the initial proceedings on the Department of Justice steps, but who is gradually caught by the tension of the possible danger that the March may offer the following day. He is not called upon to give a speech on the steps and so is forced to create for himself a central role in the gathering. His reflections on the incongruous assortment of young men who burn their draft cards corroborates the personal forboding felt by the protagonist: 'he had known from the beginning it could disrupt his life for a season or more, and in some way the danger was there it could change him forever'.(89) When Mailer moves on to the description of the March itself, he consolidates the status of his protagonist as cultural spokesman. As he and Robert Lowell walk from the Washington Monument to the Lincoln Memorial, the ghosts of the Civil War are evoked in a dramatic progression that is not fanciful but authoritative. In a long passage which vividly categorises the bizarre varieties of dress, the protagonist is now the General. As he concludes, by exclaiming 'wine of Civil War apples in the October air! edge of excitement and awe— how would this day end? No one could know . . .'.(105) his rhetoric creates a well-orchestrated fictional suspense because it functions as a political barometer, whose authority is corroborated by events enacted in the grandiose description of the troops.

Mailer, however, immediately introduces alternative personae for his protagonist in order to transform the spectacle that formerly evoked an eccentric nobility. As his point of view zooms in from the general display to a detailed closeup, he is no longer the man of action but the novelist who is unable to bear the sacrifice of individuality to any mass cause. After the Participant, who views with horror the multitude that jostle behind these signs, 'wasn't so certain that there weren't too many people alive already',(107) the Ruminant quietly concludes that 'the mediocre middle-class middle-aged masses of the Left were . . . the first real champions of technology land: they could not conceive of a revolution without hospitals, lawyers, mass meetings, and leaflets to pass out at the polls'.(ibid) Mailer avoids any suggestion of inconsistency or insincerity in effecting the rapid transformation of a protagonist who is both committed and yet uninvolved, because the personae are palpably justified by the vivid physical context which Mailer's prose carefully and skilfully establishes.

As the protagonist moves towards the climax of the March's proceedings, which is his arrest, he consolidates the duality of his removed and involved relationship with the events that surround him. Just as the presence of the author is introduced in the interaction of a reflective and active stylist, so the presence of the actor is introduced in the interaction of a subjective and objective point of view which intersect as the protagonist crosses the Military Police Line.

> It was as if the air had changed, or light had altered; he felt immediately much more alive—yes, bathed in air—and yet disembodied from himself, as if indeed he were watching himself in a film where this action was taking place. He could feel the eyes of the people behind the rope watching him, could feel the intensity of their existence as spectators.(142)

By creating a tense dramatic exchange between the mass of demonstrators and the protagonist, Mailer verifies the symbolic significance of this single act.

But before he goes on to develop this in his protagonist's reflections while in jail, Mailer digresses in order to explain that there is a point of view recording this acting which is not under his control. Mailer had allowed Dick Fontaine, a BBC director, to film his activities, although the anti-Vietnam demonstration was then an unknown factor. Fontaine went on to call his film which revolved around the events of the weekend in Washington, 'Will The Real Norman Mailer Please Stand Up'. Its chronology is similar to Book One of *The Armies of the Night*, opening with the speech at the Ambassador Theatre and closing with Mailer's speech to reporters outside Occoquan. As a result, Leiterman, Fontaine's cameraman, relieves the protagonist of the task of independently recording his activities. After establishing that Leiterman's camera has been studiously filming the arrest, he offers another version of the event which eliminates any necessity of incorporating an audience's reactions, but which belies the consciousness of that audience's presence. Just as the participant anxiously gauged the comparative response which himself and Lowell were able to evoke at the Ambassador Theatre, so now his momentous act has no value unless he can incorporate the display that the event provokes. If the first performance, which centres upon 'a clown of an *arriviste* baron',(52) presents the protagonist as a 'ludicrous figure',(51) the second allows the participant a 'not un-heroic'(148) status. He begins by withdrawing all of his many roles in order to make a pronouncement of complete subjectivity:

> He felt as if he were being confirmed . . . now he felt important in a new way. He felt his own age, forty-four, felt it as if he were finally one age, not seven, felt as if he were a solid embodiment of bone, muscle, flesh, and vested substance, rather than the will, heart, mind and sentiment to be a man, as if he had arrived, as if this picayune arrest had been his Rubicon.(149)

This dense physicality however immediately gives way once more to a preoccupation with the style of the actor which assumes rather than describes an assessing audience: 'He was secretly altogether pleased with himself at how well he has managed his bust—no cracks on the head, no silly scenes—he was damned if he was going to spoil it with an over-intense speech now, no, just the dry salient statement . . . ("I was arrested for transgressing a police line")'. (ibid) By now, the protagonist has established so well his right to claim a cultural significance for his part in these proceedings that he can afford to direct only a sidelong covert glance at the objective recorder of this scene.

When the protagonist, after his arrest, is removed from the

surveillance of reporters, Leiterman's camera and the mass of other demonstrators, his narrative must incorporate a less sympathetic audience. The transference that is effected in the protagonist in order to cope with the marshals, jailers and fellow prisoners is similar to the rapid succession of personae that were earlier employed to describe the gathering of the demonstrators. In each of these confrontations, the consciousness of the protagonist is assailed in a fashion that is similar to Rojack's confrontations with Shago Martin and Oswald Kelly. He becomes an amalgam of opposing characteristics by allowing the consciousness of his antagonist to enter his own. A perfect example of this transformation, and one which sets the pattern for the succeeding confrontations, occurs with the American Nazi and the US marshal in the truck that will take them to jail. The Nazi has been staging his own counterdemonstration and directs at the protagonist the unalloyed hatred that a racist and a fascist holds for a Jewish radical. The conflict is initially conducted in a series of 'corny' imprecations that appear to polarise the two antagonists:

> 'You Jew bastard', he shouted. 'Dirty Jew with kinky hair.'
> They didn't speak that way. It was too corny. Yet he could only answer, 'You filthy Kraut'.
> 'Dirty Jew.'
> 'Kraut pig.'(154)

Yet an advantage has already been established by the protagonist that is immediately consolidated. His unspoken message to the Nazi: ' "My eyes encompass yours. My philosophy contains yours" ',(ibid) which provokes the insulting exchange, enables him to specify the point at which their philosophies converge: 'In retrospect, it would appear not uncomic—two philosophical monomaniacs with the same flaw—they could not help it, they were counterpunchers'.(ibid) The convergence of the protagonist and the Nazi is dramatically confirmed by the reaction of the marshal who is their common antagonist. Yet Mailer also allows his protagonist to appropriate the consciousness of the marshal. The violence of this marshal is not blind, inarticulate brutality but the misguided patriotism of the bigoted isolationist who is at war with 'all the subtle invisible creeping paralyses of Communism which were changing America from a land where blood was red to a land where water was foul . . .'.(155–6)

This episode is the first of a series of encounters where the protagonist, stimulated by the physical characteristics of his antagonists, is able to analyse 'the irredeemable madness of America' (162) by dramatically juxtaposing two points of view. The faces of the marshals, of stereotyped high-school kids seen from the bus or the behaviour of the prison personnel and the Commissioner all function as a key to the exploration of that section of American society of which the protagonist has no part. Yet he can understand it because he brings facets of his own various roles into play which will enable their experience and his briefly to intersect. As a one-time soldier in the US Army, he feels that he is able to speak with authority on the small-town Texan mentality that belongs to the marshals:

> It was a great deal to read on the limited evidence before him but he had known these faces before—they were not so different from the cramped, mean, stern, brave, florid, bestial, brutish, narrow, calculating, incurious, hardy, wily, leathery, simple, good, stingy, small-town faces he had once been familiar with in his outfit overseas. . . .(164)

As a man with a Southern wife and in-laws, he feels the dishonesty of simply regarding the prison personnel as his enemies: 'Some of them were nice enough to be his in-laws, some not, but he could not pretend he did not understand them, or that he must hate them because they were Southerners'.(183) In order to sympathise with the prison cleaner whose weekend has been so rudely disrupted, he actually adopts his in-laws' point of view and then goes on to reconstruct the mental process by which the prison hack expresses his resentment of the demonstrators. Yet the disclaimer that immediately follows simultaneously maintains the point of view of one of the imprisoned—'Stale thoughts. His detestation of prison came from the mark it left on the mind. He had been in the coop not twenty-four hours and his mind was already feeling stale'.(210)

The self-conscious artistry with which Mailer manipulates the various audiences in front of whom his protagonist performs is utilised with great effect in his film *Maidstone* made the following year. The protagonist chooses to incorporate into the narrative versions of his actions presented by the press and Leiterman's camera, as well as his own version which emanates from that part of

his persona which can spectate as well as act. He deliberately
decides therefore to relinquish complete control of his material until
he assembles the various versions into a coherent form that
capitalises upon the unspoken meaning of what is often incongruous juxtapositioning. Mailer's method, in filming *Maidstone,*
was to establish five camera crews who were given complete
autonomy in what they chose to film. He explains in the film to one
of the actresses his reasons for choosing this method:

> You're still thinking of movies that are made where you very
> carefully structure them. You get the maximum out of each
> moment. But what I'm arguing for in this method is that you
> cannot make a movie that way and get anything even remotely
> resembling the truth. That way you just get a unilinear abstract
> of one man's conception of how something possibly might
> happen. But what I'm saying is that that's not the way anything
> happens. The way anything happens is that we have five realities
> at any given moment . . . .(117)

The protagonist of *The Armies of the Night* eludes any single
definition of his character therefore, because the truth of the
narrative cannot be found in 'a unilinear abstract of one man's
conception'(ibid) of it.

One of the Mailer's principal objections to Bertolucci's film, *Last
Tango in Paris* was that Marlon Brando's performance was too much
of a self-indulgent display of his own 'kinks', his 'private obsessions'[15] to fit into the role of Paul, the proprietor of a cheap
flophouse. The character of Paul (which was preconceived by
Bertolucci when he intended Louis Trintignant for the part), and
the personality of Brando, therefore rest in an incongruous
juxtaposition which, according to Mailer, often renders the plot
senseless. 'Let us say that at the least Paul is close enough to the
magnetic field of Marlon for an audience to be unable to
comprehend why Jeanne would be repelled if he has a flophouse.
Who cares, if it is Marlon who invites you to live in a flophouse?'[16]
Mailer's definition of the kind of acting which would have solved
this incongruity is 'playing at a fictitious role, while using real
feelings, which then begin to serve (rather than the safety of the
script) to stimulate him into successive new feelings and responses . . .'.[17] This is exactly what Mailer achieves in his role as the
protagonist of *The Armies of the Night* and as Norman T. Kingsley in

Maidstone by adapting the individual reality of these personae to the changing collective reality that surrounds them. In *The Armies of the Night*, this distinction is defined as that between the novel and history; in *Maidstone*, it is defined as that between the psychological and the real.

Mailer divides *The Armies of the Night* into two books, the first being 'History as a Novel', the second 'The Novel as History'. It is a division that allows Mailer to supplement his own experiences on the March with a discussion of events in which he played no part but which he considers to have important repercussions to an overall analysis. Although Mailer insists, however, that his protagonist is endowed with 'more than average gifts of objectivity'(228) who is able to convert a historical event into a novel which is 'the personification of a vision which will enable one to comprehend other visions better . . .',(231) the authority of this representative vision is lost when the protagonist fades from view in Book Two. Mailer interrupts his reconstruction of events which led up to the confrontation of troops and demonstrators, with a qualification of the structural distinction that divides *The Armies of the Night*:

> . . . the first book can be, in the formal sense, nothing but a personal history which while written as a novel was to the best of the author's memory scrupulous to facts, and therefore a document; whereas the second, while dutiful to all newspaper accounts, eyewitness reports, and historic inductions available . . . is finally now to be disclosed as some sort of condensation of a collective novel . . . .(267–8)

But the fact remains that Book One is a novel by virtue of the fact that it has a protagonist who personifies a vision through the dramatic interaction of a collective and personal reality. Although Mailer insists that 'no document can give sufficient intimation' (ibid) of the events which he is about to describe in Book Two, he must still rely on newspaper reports, along with friends' accounts. 'The welter of a hundred confusing and opposed facts'(ibid) stresses what has already been established: the unreliability of second-hand reports. 'That world of strange lights and intuitive speculation' (ibid) more clearly describes Book One, where the welter of opposed facts is contained in the inner ambitions of a protagonist struggling with his 'more than average gifts of objectivity'.(228)

The form of *Maidstone* is a direct development of Book One of *The*

Armies of the Night in that Norman T. Kingsley is a persona of Mailer who demonstrates the dramatic confrontation between a personal and collective reality. In retrospect, Mailer realised that '*Maidstone* had been filmed not only as an imaginary event but as a real event, and so was both a fiction and a documentary at once'.(178) During the bulk of the film, he is obviously building the plot upon this theory. Kingsley is a director who is in the process of making a film while his Presidential ambitions are discussed by those who are speculating upon his possible assassination. Mailer deliberately blurs the boundary between the film we are watching and the film that is contained within it. His director as Presidential candidate displays characteristics that, if the histrionic intensity is discounted, are obviously shared with Mailer himself: ' "I am an actor, a director, I'm fascinated with exposing myself to multitudes. Do you understand? It's the only thing that gives me pleasure—the only thing that gives me pleasure—is to be absolutely without shame" '.(76) This is a claim that is made in the course of an interview with Doctor Adeline McCarthy, president of a ladies' college, and while Kingsley discourses to her upon the nature of Presidential power, the interview is interspersed with shots of a group of blacks demonstrating the loss of power by one of their number by virtue of the fact that he has taken a white woman. The cutting of this sequence suggests that the nature of power is being examined as it is practised by an oppressed minority group and by the President himself. Even though the actors are improvising their respective dialogues, the group of blacks illustrate Kingsley's thesis that in a time of crisis when ' "nobody, nobody alive, has any power anymore over historic events" '(70) it is necessary to utilise the power an individual can seize and manipulate, and take the risk as to the outcome of the change such power may effect.

Later in the film Mailer takes his blurred distinction between fiction and documentary one stage further. The film within a film is centred around the transactions within a male whorehouse with Kingsley playing the part of the male madame. Although Kingsley wears a madame's costume (black leather vest and short dungarees), it is nevertheless difficult to discern whether Mailer is the protagonist in his own film or Kingsley's film. His dialogue with the English actress on the spirituality of love is conducted in the context of the male whorehouse but is delivered in a manner that recalls the narcissist who is running for President. The rapid cutting of the sexual scenes that follow compounds this confusion which prompts

Mailer's rhetorical question: 'is the film quietly sliding away from any preconception of what is real and what is fictional between story and acting, as we are accustomed to divide them?'(87)

The penultimate sequence in the film portrays the director addressing his cast, but there is no doubt at this point which director the audience is watching; 'he is inside the skin of his own name. He is speaking as Norman Mailer now'.(113) Mailer is concerned to discover the attitude of his cast towards him in what has been up to this point, the climactic scene of the film: The Assassination Ball. Two groups are in mysterious operation throughout the film, both stimulated by Kingsley's drive for the Presidency. Prevention of Assassination Experiments, Control (known as PAX, C), since it ' "excites assassinations rather than prevents them" ',(46) is working against Kingsley, while the Cashbox is composed of a circle of friends that surround him. No single actor is aware of who belongs to which group, least of all Mailer. Rip Torn plays the part of Kingsley's half-brother, Raoul Rey O'Houlihan, ' "about whom there is not only enigma but a certain proclivity toward malevolence" '.(47) The Assassination Ball is obviously intended to provoke the possible plots and counterplots generated by these two organisations into overt action, but the tension in this fantastic sequence is only resolved in the hysterical outburst of Chula Mae, Kingsley's wife (played by Mailer's wife, Beverley Bentley). As Mailer analyses the Ball scenes, he admits his reluctance to lose complete control of his film, which was so obviously imminent after having allowed complete autonomy to his actors: 'You see this is a movie which involved acting which had—which could have real ends. Now I didn't—I didn't think that the real ends were going to take place, I didn't want them to take place . . . I went out there with one thought in mind. That was "Don't mess with me, mother!" ' (116–17) Rip Torn, however, violently wrenches that control from Mailer in a sequence that was hastily filmed after the rest of the company had dispersed. Carrying his conception of his role as the enigmatic, malevolent Rey to its ultimate conclusion, he attacks Kingsley, who has reverted back to Mailer, with a hammer. In the analysis of the Ball, he has told Mailer, ' "I was in constant conflict between you, Norman, as the man, and the character of Kingsley that you're playing" '.(114) After the attack, he explains:

Rip: The picture doesn't make sense without this. You know.

Norman: Fuck you, the picture doesn't make sense. (*Turns and looks at him*) It was my picture, and I knew what I was doing with it, and what makes sense, and what don't.(127)

It is this explosive final sequence which forces Mailer into the realisation that we work 'as actors in the real story of our lives, pursuing roles which can become actual lives at any instant the psychological can become the real . . . '.(179) He demonstrates the truth of this argument in his combat with the police and the press in *The Armies of the Night*. As long as his audience is sympathetic—that is, under his control—the transference of the psychological into the real is an aesthetic exercise only. When Mailer loses control of the social impact of his roles, that transference is also affected with active abruptness. There is an analogous situation to this confrontation, defined in the essay on *Maidstone* as that between the 'psychological reality'(178) and its eruption onto 'the surface of reality'(ibid) in *The Armies of the Night*. This is when Mailer's personae transform the attack on the Pentagon from a symbolic battle to one 'which might have real broken heads . . . '.(108) It is the apparent incongruity of such an event where 'the forces defending that bastion reacted as if a symbolic wound could prove as mortal as any other combative rent',(65) that renders it ambiguous. Any attempt to evaluate its meaning must, according to Mailer, necessitate a protagonist 'ambiguous in his own proportions'(64) who 'in writing his personal history of these four days' is 'delivered a discovery of what the March on the Pentagon had finally meant . . . '.(228) The Pentagon is an ideal image for the ambiguity of a March which can convert the plans for symbolic assault into actual violence and one which Mailer dramatically explores in the frequent search of his protagonist for a suitable metaphor to expose its enigma. He also, however, offers the reader an explanation of this ambiguity by diagnosing the cultural sickness of the nation as a national schizophrenia.

His conviction that the cultural decay in America finds its source in frozen ideological, artistic and spiritual incoherencies recurs in Mailer's writing from *Cannibals and Christians*, where he maintains a faith in the power of the artistic imagination to effect a reconciliation, to *Why Are We in Vietnam?* where D. J. as disc jockey confirms this frozen polarity. In *The Armies of the Night*, the protagonist sadly mocks the ability of the writer to provide an antidote. The novelist in the book enjoys only a precarious status because he must pit his art in constant competition with 'Hollywood, T.V., and *Time*'.(169) He believes that 'responsibility was for the pompous, and the public servants; writers were born to discover wine. It was an old argument and he was worn with it . . . '.(168–9) Mailer invokes the nostalgia of Wolfe, Hemingway and Fitzgerald, but since he is aware of his propensity to sentimentalise these figures, their mention remains a passing tribute to his own impasse as a novelist. There is no answer to Mailer's question 'had the two worlds of America drifted irretrievably apart?'(169) but he can define those two worlds. In his introduction to *Cannibals and Christians*, Mailer had distinguished two huge types in American society: the Cannibals and the Christians. He now asserts that both types are encapsulated within each individual American 'who was devoutly Christian and worked for the American Corporation . . .'.(200) Since the former is a mystery and the latter a detestation of mystery, individuals are 'caught in an unseen vise whose pressure could split their mind from their soul'.(ibid) Mailer therefore reiterates what he has already demonstrated in the electronic performance of D. J.'s voice: that the evil which had led to the brutalities of the war in Vietnam is within 'since the expression of brutality offers a definite if temporary relief to the schizophrenic'.(ibid)

The historian in Book Two elaborates upon the dilemma of America's polarisation by stressing the difficulty in morally evaluating the confrontation between demonstrators and troops. Although it is necessary to endorse an attack upon an elusive authority that furthers this immoral war, the historian demonstrates what is to recur in Mailer's subsequent writing again and again: that there is a lamentable but inevitable confusion in the confrontation between the revolutionary and the establishmentarian which obfuscates an evaluation of the outcome. To the protagonist of *The Armies of the Night*, however, the polarisation of American culture is not an inevitability. His arrest and its repercussions provide the key to the meaning of the March, but it is not a meaning that can be contained in a single definition or analysis (such as Mailer attempts in Book Two). It is to be found in the fluid control that the participant's ego exercises over the form of Book One. In prison he shares an uneasy relationship with Teague, who is a dedicated Leninist revolutionary. As he listens to Teague give a critique of the March, he reflects 'Doubtless there had been something wrong in the style of the move on the Pentagon, but it would take him weeks to comprehend this March, and the events now taking place . . . '.(204) But the elucidation of 'the mysterious character of that quintessentially American event'(228) which Mailer heralds as the task of Book Two is contained in Book One where the protagonist can reach beyond the author's rhetorical questions by virtue of the fact that he is a 'prisoner of his own egotism', and so 'some large vital part of the March had ended for him with his own arrest'.(204) In order to analyse the faults of the March, the protagonist would have to share Teague's ability to efface his individuality in the collective cause, would have to nurture an evangelical zeal for a revolutionary ideology which would have 'the hard firm impact of all the sound-as-brickwork-logic of the next step . . . '.(191)

The protagonist cannot do this because the March is understood as a series of personal confrontations between his own acted personae and the uncalculated response of his audience. Mailer had developed this procedure in his film-making by insisting upon the necessity of improvisation. The filming of *Maidstone* conclusively proved to him the virtues of the theory, so that in his review of *Last Tango in Paris*, Mailer offered an extensive critique of Bertolucci's film on the basis of Marlon Brando's compromised acting. Although Brando appropriates Bertolucci's original concept of the character of Paul, by providing the audience with protracted views into his own monolithic ego, the fact remains that the outline of the plot has already been drafted: 'One does not add improvisation to a script which is already written and with an ending that is locked up'.[18] Bertolucci rests his entire film on the final view of Paul, shot dead, curled like a foetus on the balcony of Jeanne's Paris apartment. No matter that Brando offers his own brilliant contribution to the sequence, which is to have Paul carefully place his chewing gum on the underside of the balcony rail before keeling over. The basic logic, as Mailer argues, is faulty. True improvisation 'should have moved forward each day on the actor's experience of the day before . . . ',[19] and so rest in the no-man's-land of a fictitious role and real feeling, between the psychological and the real or between the novel and history. The protagonist of *The Armies of the Night* constantly stresses his inability to judge 'what might be important next and what might not'(151) but in admitting as much, he personifies that faction of American society which might provide an antidote to its divisive sickness. Those who march on the Pentagon acknowledge another kind of mystery that is only marginally related to Christianity: 'Belief was reserved for the revelatory mystery of the happening where you did not know what was going to happen next; that was what was good about it'.(97–8)

During this period of prodigious activity, Mailer had apparently acted, quite literally, on the conviction that every detail of his life was crucially relevant to, and a reflection of the cultural, political and social climate of America. As a result, his work during these years fulfils the energetic conclusion of 'Some Dirt in the Talk'. If 'each year, civilization gives its delineated promise of being further coterminous with schizophrenia' then 'the aim of a robust art still remains: that it be hearty, that it be savage, that it serve to feed audiences with the marrow of its honest presence'.(122)

4 The Novelist versus The Reporter

Never again, up to the present time, have Mailer's creative performances so legitimately occupied the centre of the stage. The protagonist of *The Armies of the Night* and the director and leading actor of *Maidstone* play a starring role. In *Miami and the Siege of Chicago*, the protagonist's uncomfortable performances in the limelight are only momentary so that, as in *St George and the Godfather*, Mailer is forced to rely far more upon his skills as a prose stylist, rather than as an active participant. Yet he discovers a singular insight into the National Conventions of 1968 and 1972 by expressing a genuine bewilderment as to which role this writer should assume: that of the passive and observing reporter or that of the literary man who participates in several of the events he witnesses.

At Miami in 1968, 'The reporter had moved through the convention quietly, as anonymously as possible, wan, depressed, troubled'.[1] To be a satisfactory political reporter, one must be able to detect the manoeuvres for power, and Mailer is weary of the technical gymnastics through which he must put his reporter in order to describe an event coherently, when its outward manifestation so little accords with its inner workings. Gary Wills has correctly remarked that 'you have to get on stage to catch Mailer's eye'[2] and indeed, at Miami 'one could not tell if nothing much was going on, or to the contrary, nothing much was going on near the surface but everything was shifting down below'.(14) Nixon's prenomination press conference bewilders the reporter who attended with firm preconceptions about the candidate's hypocrisy. He can only counter the inadequacy of his observations with an inappropriate return to his cosmic oppositions: 'New and marvellously complex improvement of a devil, or angel-in-chrysalis, or both—good and evil now at war in the man, Nixon was at least, beneath the near to hermetic boredom of his old presence, the most interesting figure at the convention . . .'.(49) The limp observation that qualifies this grand statement illustrates the uncertain relationship between Mailer and his persona which he so vehemently gives voice to in *A Fire on the Moon*(1970). It is this uncertainty which occasions the crucial nature of his reaction to the assassination of Bobby Kennedy. After watching the television for news of Kennedy's condition 'he went back to bed and lay in a sweat of complicity, as if his own lack of moral *witness* . . . could be found in the dance of evasions his taste for a merry life and a married one had become . . .'.(91–2) Unlike the spouse of the protagonist of *The Armies of the Night*, who is both an image and a literal reality, the reporter's wife is simply a woman who cannot possibly be accused of an indirect complicity in this national tragedy. Mailer and his reporter are not sufficiently distinct to prevent the concluding reflection of this episode from being a maudlin fantasy. 'Who knew what in reality might have been granted if he had worked for the first impulse and dared offer confession on a connubial bed. A good could have come to another man and by another route'.(93)

These are temporary lapses, however, in Mailer's book on the Conventions of 1968. The events are described by a narrator who is struggling to maintain a professionally objective stance against a natural reluctance to remain in the audience. Because the political figures perform so badly before the spectator, he experiences a desire to seek the limelight which his professional self knows will be detrimental to his task of illuminating the events. Each press conference, publicity speech, social gathering and arrival is dutifully attended by the reporter, who cannot assess whether the theatricality of the politicians' speeches is a mark of insincerity or versatility. Mailer's achievement is to suggest convincingly that the enigma of the politician finds its source in the narrator who is struggling to present himself in sharp focus as the form of his narrative unfolds. The reporter seizes upon each publicly delivered speech and by closely analysing the connotations of each word or phrase, with his interpolated reactions which are suggested by the performed delivery, the speaker is incorporated into the spectator. Waiting to listen to the Reverend Ralph Abernathy speak on Black rights, the reporter's irritation grows as he contemplates the aggressive arrogance that Abernathy's tardiness suggests to him. Although he chides himself that as 'a reporter who must attempt to do his job, he had perhaps committed himself too completely to the atmosphere as if better to comprehend the subterranean character of what he saw on the surface . . .',(50) he nevertheless feels confounded as to the nature of the Black rebellion, which appears offensive in its exploiting tyranny, so that 'he must have become in some secret part of his flesh a closet Republican . . .'.(52) Abernathy does not relieve the reporter's anxiety because, like his observer, he is never in focus. The reporter practically demonstrates the blurred outline of speaker-and-auditor by reproducing extracts of Abernathy's speech, stressing the sound, which is lacking in conviction, rather than the content. As the reporter leaves, his weariness at 'confronting the mystery of his own good or ill motive'(55) describes Abernathy as well as himself.

Richard Nixon taxes the reporter's ingenuity to the full. He is obsessed with him because his picture of the man had not allowed for the possibility of the phoenix rising from the ashes of political defeat. The reporter's version of Nixon's first speech exposes the lies behind the latter's false sincerity. Like Abernathy, Nixon moves in and out of the reporter's focus, until he assumes the part of a puppet whose strings are manipulated by the spectator. When Nixon delivers his acceptance speech, the reporter is again caught in the dilemma of assessing Nixon. The sound of his voice echoes sentiments that suggest the calculation of a computer, which renders the role of the reporter superfluous.

After a constant feeling of disquiet at his inability to place the speakers in any comprehensible focus, the reporter realises the nature of his problem while attending a debate between McGovern, Humphrey and McCarthy. During Humphrey's extended speech and question-and-answer session, he understands that Humphrey's insincerity is caused by the fact that the latter 'simply could not attach the language of his rhetoric to any reality; on the contrary, he was perfectly capable of using the same word, "Freedom" let us say, to describe a ward fix in Minneapolis and a gathering of Quakers'.(120) The reporter's mistake has been to assume that on stage, the selfhood of the politician is identical to his offstage personality. He settles into a proper sense of his role as spectator when he observes that while Humphrey spoke 'the sensation of truth quivered about him like a nimbus. He must have felt bathed in light. He had the same kind of truth that an actor has while playing Napoleon—with the lights on him, he *is* Napoleon'.(121) This, according to Mailer's theories of acting, is false consciousness. The actor must always be aware of that delicate, hardly definable boundary which separates day-to-day life from the roles he assumes.

As a result, when Humphrey is nominated for President at the Democratic Convention in Chicago, the reporter can transform his subject by concentrating upon the physical characteristics of Humphrey's public role. He 'had a face which was as dependent upon cosmetics as the protagonist of a coffin'.(201) But in *St George and the Godfather*, Aquarius amplifies that image. His minute description of Humphrey's face, clothes, wife, and mannerisms create, through a wealth of allusions, a compound image of physical decay and disintegration that constantly directs the reader's attention to his moral duplicity: 'Quickly someone asked about California. Humphrey's answer was unctuous, cynical, sincere and wicked all at once, as if the separate parts of his face were no longer flesh so much as jointed shells'.(17) Aquarius concludes not by simply undermining the sincerity of Humphrey's policies, but the reality of Humphrey himself. He has literally become a ridiculous puppet at the mercy of Mailer's prose; a 'shattered, glued, and jolly work of art, a Renaissance priest of the Vatican who could not even cross a marble floor without pieties issuing from his skirt'.(19)

Because Aquarius begins his account of the 1972 Conventions with a developed awareness of this insight into the politicians' performances, he accepts his modest status. The Democratic Convention, however, is boring to Aquarius because it is dominated by George McGovern who is not an actor, but a 'living embodiment of a principle which was only new to the Age of Technology: the clear expectation of democratic government that good and serious men of honorable will were ready to serve'.(112) The manoeuvres for power are hidden from Aquarius, because they are concealed by a bland innocence which is a stranger to the duplicities of the actor. Aquarius' reporting vocation therefore is not that of a factually accurate recorder but an appreciative critic of the public perform-ance. It is not important to know the details of a convention's evasory tactics but rather to have 'the skill . . . to read the moves of a convention' when 'the posture of political fixes came out in the set of the hips when a deal was in . . .'.(86) To Aquarius, a convention must be a dramatic performance in order that an understanding of its participants might be reached. At the Democratic Convention, George Wallace is the exception that proves the rule. Watching Wallace arrive in Miami, Aquarius notes how the politician has turned his physical disability to advantage. His dignity is em-phasised by the controlled fear of his helplessness, and Aquarius admires this new self-creation. 'If every politician is an actor, only a few are consummately talented. Wallace is talented'.(15) For the first time, he understands a public figure and as a result '[Wallace] is the first note of the real that Aquarius has encountered at this convention, and his presence, a work of art, remains in the back of the mind . . .'.(ibid)

Because Aquarius is able to discover 'the promise of design'(137) in the unfolding of the Republican Convention, he calls it the 'Nixon Spectacular'.(185) Despite the fact that this Spectacular is constructed purely for the camera eye, Aquarius is sensitive enough to the mechanics of political stage-managing to discover the organisation behind the smooth façade. At the Sunday Worship Service, he surveys the congregation and realises the pervasive intelligence of Nixon in the carefully balanced assortment of ethnic, regional and social representatives. At the Convention itself, he calls this 'the Jeannette Weiss Principle . . . wherever possible use a black lady with a German Jewish name doing a patriotic bit' and concludes that 'It is the mark of great artists that they pay attention to those surfaces of the work to the rear of the niche'.(180–1) Aquarius does not require the physical presence of Nixon to know that he is not only a genius (to demonstrate 'that a politician who was fundamentally unpopular even in his own party could nonetheless win the largest free election in the world, and give every promise of doing considerably better the second time!') but an artist, 'who had discovered the laws of vibration in all the frozen congelations of the mediocre'.(137–8) The reporter who, in *Miami and the Siege of Chicago*, sat before a television screen in sad confusion at his lack of intimation 'of what was in a politician's heart'(80) has developed, in *St George and the Godfather*, into Aquarius who, with his intimate understanding of Nixon's acting talents, does not need the physical figure of the man before him to appropriate his logic. Indeed, Nixon only enters the narrative in its later stage when he is likened to a puppet and an array of oscillating dots on the television screen. His most palpable presence is found in the series of pungent pronouncements entitled *Nixon's Maxims* which are created by Aquarius-turned-Nixon. The function of these maxims is to counter the assumed warmth and sincerity of Nixon's public image with a private cynicism that fosters an understanding of his courtship of the silent majority. This cynicism is couched in a parodied version of Nixon's style. The context of each maxim highlights the pervasive dishonesty of a demagogic government. After the portrait of Agnew as a shrewd and self-centred man, the maxim states that the silent majority will vote 'for anything which suggests the maintenance of their daily life. Let me say that the more this daily life is without interest, the harder they will vote'.(175) Daniel Ellsberg's passionate denouncement of the American bombing of Vietnam and Cambodia is concluded by a steely pronouncement on the manipulation of public opinion.

> The Silent Majority, while often accused of being non-political, actually prefer to have a definite idea and will often drift at surprising speed from one position to its opposite. May I point to the shift of opinion on the war in Vietnam. The American public once ready to get out is now ready to stay in and win provided no American blood is shed.(196)

Similarly, Aquarius laconically resorts to the creative imagination of his persona to counter the blandness of Republican management who isolate their exhibition of the Vice-President behind a velvet rope in an art museum on the outskirts of Miami. The theory of 'psychotronics, the new science of the century' that puts Aquarius 'on the same beam of RN Maxim Intuits that the Nixon staff was receiving'(171) is a comic device with a serious function. The reader is reminded that the dialogue between the Republican aides is an invention by the frustrated narrator, which enables him to discover, by means of this released creativity, the essence of Spiro Agnew. The process of discovery involves the powers of the reporter and the literary man. Aquarius casts a careful eye over the details of the galleries, pillars, arches and Italian steps of Vizcaya and the dark suit, white shirt, black-and-white tie and heavy-lidded eyes of Agnew while simultaneously searching for the correct image that will encapsulate the mood and meaning of such a scene. It is only when the reporter notices the pocked look of the coral out of which the flagstones have been made that his creative imagination can reach for the associations occasioned by the idea of bullet-holes.

> Agnew's suit assumes its focus. He looks, of course! he looks like he is wearing just the suit a Latin American dictator would wear in his palace by the tropical sea, and indeed has there ever been a man as high in American public life who has looked this much like the general who throws over a banana republic in a putsch?(173)

The imagination of Aquarius controls the narrative drama, not the action of Spiro Agnew, so that when the image is qualified as being too simple for a 'curious fellow'(ibid) like Agnew, it is not the complexity of Agnew that is being celebrated, but the complexity of Aquarius perceiving Agnew. On the television 'Agnew had looked merely like Agnew. Now, ten feet away, across the untransmitted air, there was this inexplicable sense of his privacy as if no one in America knew the first thing about him'.(174) Mailer concludes the episode with an image that is remarkable for its compressed meaning. It is an apparently frustrated reporter who departs the scene recording a tableau that is peripheral to the main event: 'the cops are feasting in the wood on what is left of the sandwiches in the rain'.(ibid) But it is the literary imagination which has discerned the wealth of implication in this small detail. The notion of 'cops' feasting in a wood carries connotations of the sinister ogre in a Gothic melodrama, which is abruptly deflated by the prosaically depressing remains of soggy sandwiches. It expresses Aquarius' maintained conviction that the essence of Republicanism is always this exact combination of elaborately sinister melodrama and depressingly prosaic conventionality.

In *Miami and the Siege of Chicago*, the absence of a connection between language and reality which the reporter observes in Humphrey's performance has repercussions when he is faced with obligations to occupy the active arena himself. While he is a member of the audience, he remains a reporter no matter how inefficiently he practises his professional duties. When he faces the revolutionary youth groups in Lincoln Park, Chicago, however, he realises that the discrepancy between a word and its reality has disturbing implications. The reporter is also a literary man who is confronted with an obligation not only to witness and record the protest of the police order to leave the park at 11.00 pm, but to participate actively in it. Yet there must be a symbol to push the literary man into action. In Washington, he marched against the Pentagon, which effectively symbolised the hated military–industrial complex. In Chicago, there is no connection between the word Vietnam and its connotations of national immorality, and the ridiculous open-ended barricade built against the police. 'This symbolic contest with real bloody heads'(143) seems therefore pointless.

When the young protestors meet the arbitrary brutality of the Chicago police, the narrator retreats to his hotel room on the nineteenth floor and views the violence which, from this vantage point, appears to be incredibly beautiful:

> there was something of the detachment of studying a storm at evening through a glass, the light was a lovely gray-blue, the police had uniforms of sky-blue, even the ferocity had an abstract elemental play of forces of nature at battle with other forces, as if sheets of tropical rain were driving across the street in patterns, in curving patterns which curved upon each other again.(164)

The distanced appreciation that this violent scene occasions is similar to Mailer's explanation to Paul Krassner in 'An Impolite Interview', of Ciano, Mussolini's son-in-law, who found the explosion of a bomb viewed from the air a beautiful sight: ' "This act of perception was *not* what was wrong; the evil was to think that this beauty was worth the lot of living helpless people who were wiped out broadside" '.(150) The sight of the brutality in Michigan Avenue is a turning point in *Miami and the Siege of Chicago*. After this, the narrator must examine the truth of Mailer's argument to Paul Krassner, and, as a result, the narrative is presented by a point of view that struggles between the role of the reporter as spectator and the participating literary man. After the description from the hotel window, versions of the event are quoted from reporters who are caught in the confrontation. Their descriptions are filled with shock and horror at the atrocities they have witnessed, but the narrator describes it with the detachment of a theatre spectator: 'Look—a boy was running through the park, and a cop was chasing. There he caught him on the back of the neck with his club! There! The cop is returning to his own! And the boy stumbling to his feet is helped off the ground by a girl who has come running up.'(167)

The narrator dutifully returns to the scene of the Convention where he describes the events that lead up to the nomination of Hubert Humphrey. When a caucus of McCarthy delegates silently march with candles to the Conrad Hilton Hotel to protest the violence of Mayor Daley's police, the reporter again retreats from the possibility of his own involvement in an action that could end in beatings. He justifies his evasion by discussing his professional deadline, but the self-disgust of the literary man constantly intrudes. Guiding his narrative back to the spectacle viewed from the hotel window, the narrator is confused as to which role he owes his allegiance. 'He was simply not accustomed to living with a conscience as impure as the one with which he had watched from the nineteenth floor. Or had it really been impure? Where was his true engagement?'(182) Step by step, the tension drifts away from the social drama in Lincoln Park and towards the inner drama between the narrator's two selves. Should he commit himself, as the writer, to a personal involvement with the troops in the park or confine himself to the skill of the reporter who, as a spectator, can appropriate the performing techniques of the political protagonists? The narrator now reveals the agony of his decision to speak at the meeting in Grant Park prior to the march down Michigan Avenue. As a writer, he weakly asks himself that if national life is so disrupted by these protests as to destroy the lifestyle to which he is accustomed 'Was he ready to give up the pleasures of making his movies, writing his books? They were pleasures finally he did not want to lose'.(ibid) But he then wryly returns to his role as a detached witness:

> These are large thoughts for a reporter to have. Reporters live happily removed from themselves. They have eyes to see, ears to hear, and fingers for the note in their report. It was as if the drink he took in now moved him millimeter by millimeter out from one hat into another. He would be driven yet to participate or keep the shame in his liver . . . .(182-3)

He had rediscovered the pleasures of the performer earlier that afternoon by addressing Dellinger's meeting, because 'he was finally enough of an actor to face perils on a stage he would not meet as quickly other ways'.(184) Yet the narrator's brief experience as an active performer is always qualified by the evasory tactics of the reporter. As a writer he rejoins the troops in Michigan Avenue and delivers another speech, culminating in his request for two hundred delegates to march with him to the Amphitheatre where the Convention has taken place. But with the failure of his plan to march, the sense of loss occasioned by the disappearance of the literary man who was prepared to instigate an action capable of illuminating or possibly influencing the Convention proceedings is matched by the emptiness of the reporter at Humphrey's nomination.

In *St George and the Godfather*, however, Aquarius does not experience this dilemma when wandering through Flamingo Park, which is occupied by demonstrators against the Republicans. Aquarius knows that his skill as a reporter will enable him to write subjectively of the Convention proceedings without losing his professional detachment. This detachment is solidly, even cheerfully maintained as he views Flamingo Park from the balcony of a twelfth-floor hotel room.

> He must have turned some corner in his life for he feels no shame whatsoever. Later he will go out and eat a good dinner and not think of the kids in the park. When the time came for the real war, if it ever came, and came to America, he would presumably be enough of a man to recognize it. If he was not, it would be his own karmic ass he fried.(168)

Aquarius maintains the literal and symbolic vantage point that the reporter so shamefacedly resorted to in Chicago. When the street action of the youth groups results in retaliation from the police in the form of tear gas, Aquarius joins the streets in order to describe the scattered incidents among the divided and disorganised demonstrations. His task is firmly dedicated to the study of Republican concepts, however. The Left-wing militants have reached an impasse in their attack on the establishment, so that 'the smell of dead drugs is like the smell of old green bills'.(220) Aquarius views the rising moon emerging from the drifting tear gas as he watches 'the action from the vast roof of a vast parking garage' and muses on his emotion. This action is 'sad and absurd and pointless and lost and will not save a life in Vietnam, and yet he loves it, loves Miami Beach to his amazement, this crazy city of permissions and symbolic wars . . .'.(226)

Although Aquarius has abdicated from involvement in militant Left-wing protest action and although the reporter in Chicago had finally to witness the impotence of the active man of letters, there is a constant moral urgency in both of Mailer's narrative dramas. In *Miami and the Siege of Chicago*, the narrator assesses the compromise in the reporter's professional commitment:

> The reporter knew he had much to write about, but could he now enjoy writing it?
>   Sometimes he thought that the rate of one's ability to do good writing day after day was a function of good conscience. A professional could always push a work by an exercise of will, yet

was writing himself right out of his liver if the work was obliged to protect the man.(206–7)

Yet the climax of the narrative is an exposure of the reporter's crisis of conscience. The image of the aerial spectator also functions, in both *Miami and the Siege of Chicago* and *St George and the Godfather*, to expose the desolate impotence of street warfare. He enjoys a view that is theoretically available to any pair of eyes that search for and take advantage of such a vantage point. Yet the narrator in *Miami and the Siege of Chicago* describes the swirling pattern of troop-fighting below in an image that stresses the lack of control both sides have over their confrontations. The reporter and Aquarius utilise their removed point of view to discover an insight that is not immediately apparent. Because each vivid cameo of street violence is created by a point of view that has learned the hopelessness of guerrilla street fighting, the theatrical nature of each confrontation reflects the impossibility of simply offering partisan sympathy. It is the fact of violence, not simply the brutality of the Chicago police or the issue of trashing the police versus protesting the war in Vietnam, that is repugnant.

The narrators of *Miami and the Siege of Chicago* and *St George and the Godfather* recognise that their role is to try to understand by intuition the nature of politics as it is practised on the Convention floor. At the reception for Republican delegates in 1968, the reporter forcibly recognises his lack of partisan bias as he observes that the power of the nation should be fairly placed in the hands of the WASPs until the Left had learned 'through a species of political exile . . . what was alive in the conservative dream'.(62) Throughout *Miami and the Siege of Chicago* with the exception of his futile attempt to organise a march on the Amphitheatre, the reporter stands 'in the center of the American Scene',(63) because neither Left nor Right-wing ideology bears any relevance to the essence of politics. As the reporter and Aquarius move through the conventions of 1968 and 1972, they learn that party politics is grounded upon expedient concepts that eliminate the individual and individual confrontation. The narrators counter this with their reluctant but sincere sympathy for individual delegates with whom they have no ideological empathy. At the Republican gala in 1968, the reporter concludes from a detailed observation of the physique of the guests that 'there was the muted tragedy of the Wasp—they were not on earth to enjoy or even perhaps to love so very much, they were here to serve, and

serve they had in public functions and public charities . . .'.(35) At
the Republican Convention 1972, Aquarius reads the faces of the
delegates:

> He saw faces which were models of discipline, or of elegance, or
> orderly style, faces which spoke of fire and pride and the idea that
> character was the only ceramic to hold human fire and pride;
> there were dry Republican faces which proved models of
> crystallized wit, and kindly urbane gentlemen whose minds were
> rich with concept when they thought of the common-weal.(207)

The narrators' appropriation of these individuals by means of their
physical rather than ideological characteristics enables them to
understand the delegates' need for a leader.

The fascination that Mailer had with Kennedy, who could
combine conventional and individualist leadership, directs his
narrators to feel contempt for both Democratic and Republican
politicians, who have dehumanised the nature of political
manoeuvring. In 'Superman comes to the Supermarket', Mailer
euphorically described the Democratic Convention in 1960 as
'meeting, feud, vendetta, conciliation, of rabblerousers, fist fights
(as it used to be), embraces, drunks (again as it used to be) and
collective rivers of animal sweat'(66) which recalled the fact that
the hygiene of high politics had roots that 'still come grubby from
the soil . . . '.(ibid) Yet in a prefatory remark in *The Presidential
Papers*, in the aftermath of John Kennedy's assassination, he
recorded the results of the disappearance of this personal
confrontation.

> Today, a successful politician is not a man who wrestles with the
> art of the possible in order to enrich life, alleviate hardship, or
> correct injustice—he is, on the contrary, a doctor of mass
> communications who may measure his success by the practice of a
> political ritual and vocabulary which diverts us temporarily from
> dread, from anxiety, from the mirror of the dream.(166)

The narrators of *Miami and the Siege of Chicago* and *St George and the
Godfather* give several versions of this expedient degeneration, which
serve as a key to the performances of the Conventions' actors. In
1968, the reporter expounds his theory of politics as property which
reduces a politician to being an unscrupulous servant 'of ideological

institutions or interests and the available moral passions of the electorate . . . You pick up as much as you can, pay the minimum for the holding, extract the maximum, and combine where you may . . . '.(103) Beginning with Lyndon Johnson as the pioneer of this unworthy philosophy, the reporter traces the desperate moves of Humphrey who, without the basic property of his seat as Senator, is the pawn of Johnson and the Hawks and therefore possesses no political selfhood to justify his move to seize the nomination. The reporter returns again and again to the idea of politics as property, which suggests his bitter sense of discovery at the shift of emphasis from individually held convictions to expediently manipulated concepts. In 1972, Aquarius appropriates the spirit of party politics in order to provide, aphoristically, working definitions that a politician, suspended in a vacuum between a word and its reality, would be unwilling or unable to provide. His delight is to express in tersely direct statements what the candidates unwittingly demonstrate in their expedient manoeuvres, which expose a combination of ineptness and Machiavellian cunning.

Before arriving at the 1972 Democratic Convention, Aquarius announces his heretical conviction that 'he had an absolute disbelief in political argument' because 'politics was a game in which points were scored and one tried to obscure the depth and gravity of the process'.(5) Government should be 'as intimate as carnal relations'(6) yet the individual politican wilfully obfuscates this fact. Muskie is derided as pitiful and incompetent in his courtship of the Chairman of the party because he fails to follow a rule which Aquarius takes from party politics and presents with humourously excruciating directness: 'Politics is not an art of principles but of timing. The principles are few and soft enough to curve to political winds. The fundamental action of politics is to gain the most one can from a favorable situation and pay off as little as possible whenever necessity forces an unpopular line'.(38) The aphoristic pen of Aquarius as philosopher-of-the-party becomes even more contemptuous of McGovern's frantic search for a Vice-President, which suggests the view 'that politicans should not be morally better than other men so much as more skilful'.(80) The impatience with which Aquarius concludes his report on the Democratic Convention rests on his contention that there has been insufficient evil, which 'was the law of politics and the provender of the floor'.(87) Evil, in this context, is not the boring expediency which he has witnessed, nor the sinister spectacular of the Nixon epic. It is the motivating force behind the raucous carnival that Mailer witnessed in 1960, when the Democrats nominated John Kennedy. Evil is the positive force that a natural leader, a man with charisma, manipulates in order to seize the power that bubbles and surges around him. In the course of the decade, Mailer has charted the decline of national politics in the shift of the politician from a man manipulating other men by means of his adroit skill as an actor, to men manipulated by concepts.

Nevertheless, the narrators conduct a search for a charismatic leader who will qualify that decline. Given the nature of politics whose essence has so cynically been defined, the private and public man has been irrevocably polarised. This is illustrated quite clearly in the personal confrontations that take place between the narrators and the politicians in these two books. Eugene McCarthy is a personal friend, who, in private conversation during the 1968 Democratic Convention, feels to the reporter like a President, but only after he had 'relinquished the very last of his hopes, and so was enjoying his dinner'.(127) As a public man, he must decline to meet the sacrifice of his selfhood to disembodied concepts so that 'there wasn't that sense of a man with vast ambition and sufficient character to make it luminous, so there was not that charisma which leaves no argument about the nature of the attempt'.(96) After interviewing Eagleton during the 1972 Democratic Convention, Aquarius feels a bemused contempt for a man whose obvious weakness can convert a reporter into an active embodiment of the charisma which was formerly reserved for public leaders. His interview with McGovern founders on the realisation that he has 'no real questions to ask. There was no form of inquiry on earth more unwholesome to him than a face-to-face interview—truth could emerge no more easily from that than statistics on the sum of British Guiana's arable acreage, gotten up for a test, might bring some cognition of life in British Guiana'.(110–11) Even though it concludes on a note of love for the 'good and serious men of honorable will' who 'were ready to serve',(112) it does not eliminate the vacuum of McGovern's public image which provides no distinction from Nixon's exercise of leadership—'For both men project that same void of charisma which can prove more powerful than charisma itself, although vastly less agreeable . . . '.(23)

Kissinger, on the other hand, forces Aquarius to recognise another kind of charisma. The conversation over lunch, prior to the 1972 Republican Convention, had been arranged as a formal interview, but the immediate empathy between two men so physically alike confounds Aquarius' preconceptions about Kissinger.

> Because Kissinger opened to him a painful question on the value of the act of witness: lunch had been agreeable. Yet how could one pretend that Kissinger was a man whose nature could be assessed by such a meeting; in this sense, he was not knowable . . . If there was a final social need for Establishment, then Kissinger was a man born to be part of it and so automatically installed in the moral schizophrenia of Establishment, a part of the culture of moral concealment, and yet never was the problem so perfect, for the schizophrenia had become Aquarius' own.(120)

Characteristically, Aquarius appropriates his subject, who is an apparent antagonist and, by a lengthy internal debate, transforms his persona into an amalgam of opposing viewpoints.

The crucial criterion for Aquarius, however, remains the public image. His interview with McGovern confirms the latter's courage but does not eliminate Aquarius' conviction that McGovern and the three astronauts who travelled to the moon in 1969, are public heroes who operate in a vacuum. Their courage is unrelated to circumstance, they lack a self-conscious technique which, to a Mailer protagonist, is profoundly disturbing. Mailer's notion of heroism has always been allied to the performance of the con-summate actor whose (sometimes monstrous) ego evades a final and complete definition. Whether through the personification of rapidly changing ideas, performance of voices, literary styles or styles of action, Mailer describes the hero in *The Presidential Papers* as 'the one kind of man who *never* develops by accident . . . a hero is a consecutive set of brave and witty self-creations'.(16) Armstrong, Aldrin and Collins are simply the figureheads of an organisation blindly pushing into space. Mailer's account of the moon shot therefore contains not only a struggle with his own established literary ego, but also releases a general and more crucial issue which is linguistic and ultimately cultural. When he discovers the verbal banality of all NASA employees and, most shockingly, the as-tronauts themselves, Aquarius counters his alarm and depression with the reflection 'there might not be time to develop men to speak like Shakespeare as they departed on heavenly ships'.[3] It is a

statement of ironic hyperbole, but the implications of the idea have
already been carefully examined, using Armstrong as a suggestive
illustration. Because he 'did not brandish an ego one could
perceive on meeting', it is 'as if finally he had such huge respect for
words that they were tangible omens and portents, zephyrs and
beasts of psychic presence . . .'.(26)

Aquarius' perception gives his assignment an unfamiliar character. Because there is no verbal style which he can incorporate as his
own, he feels, as a member of the Press, a horror at the lack of
reverberation from such a momentous event. The magical grandeur
behind the wall of impersonal technologese is not simply a flight of
desperate fancy on the part of Aquarius, because he builds his
studies and speculations upon personae which, in their juxtapositioning, intimate 'that reality was not what it appeared to be, not
altogether'.(130) The astronauts' linguistic blandness veils an
inchoate but profound longing for the hitherto undiscovered, their
lack of personal motivation conceals a 'first revelation of the real
intent of History'(122) because, while the familiar ego of the
reporter is loudly and ineffectually struggling with his recalcitrant
material, the novelist is transforming this blind, gargantuan push
into a project of grand cultural purpose.

The ebullient reportorial ego controls the technical surface of *A
Fire on the Moon*. His reactions to the interviews that he manages to
secure, and to the three inaccessible astronauts are all reported in a
style which employs familiar strategies, but which steadfastly fails to
function in the context of NASA and its personnel. In his first
encounter with the astronauts, the reporter is obliged to be
subsumed in the collective body of the Press. As the public interview
proceeds, he makes some effort to be a distinctive member of the
audience but the result is unconvincing. His speculations that
Armstrong 'was apparently in communion with some string in the
universe others did not think to play',(20) that Aldrin 'gave off in his
air of unassailable solemnity some incommunicable speech about
the depth of men's souls'(22) are tentative forays from a collective
mood that he cannot help but share with his associates. The Press
are bored, frustrated and resentful. Because an event of such
dimensions has nothing to offer their professional pens, it appears
that 'the relation of everyone to each other and to the event was not
quite real'.(18) But to the reporter the key to understanding this
event is always the astronauts, so that despite his reluctance, his
knowledge that it is 'idiotic', he allows himself to drift with the rest of

the Press to the Manned Spacecraft Operations Building for a last brief glimpse of Armstrong, Aldrin and Collins. He finds that they seem to possess the air of condemned men; a perception that appears to be shared by other spectators. An Italian girl repeats ' "fenomenal!" ' and an MSOB worker shouts ' "Go get 'em" '.(71) The trip begins to resemble, however faintly, a form of combat, since at that moment the moon is revealed as 'an enemy, an intimate competitor'.(72) But it is a briefly held conviction. For once, the reporter is almost wholly dependent for his insights upon the reactions of the audience, rather than upon the words or actions of the astronauts themselves. Falling back upon his own reflections, he tells himself that the paucity of simple human witness can be overcome, but this is not achieved until Aquarius abandons his reportorial persona. It remains, of course, hovering over the surface of the book, an egotistical first person that constantly acts as a master of ceremonies pointing to an unobstrusive detective. This detective, whose performance earns him the title of novelist, has a cumulative effect that transforms the notion of egotism from the professional efforts of a reporter to the personal account of a private citizen.

The transformation of Aquarius is the result of his concern with form: the form of the moon trip which is ultimately, of course, his concern with literary form. At its simplest, form, to Aquarius, is the tangible shape of a thing or the abstract shape of an idea or project, which deceives. In a fanciful meditation upon the lunar landscape, he concludes that 'not all form reveals, form may also be designed to betray meaning'.(237–8) The betrayed meaning of the moon trip is expressed by the anguished Aquarius who asks again and again 'Was the voyage of Apollo 11 the noblest expression of a technological age, or the best evidence of its utter insanity?'(310) This is the voice of the reporter, bewildered at the deception practised upon his senses. In a quieter mood, his resentment still burns as he finds that he 'was in no Command Module preparing to go around the limb of the moon, burn his rocket motors and brake into orbit, no, Aquarius was installed in the act of writing about the efforts of other men . . .'.(238) Forced into the position of thwarted observer, he can discover nothing rational in the moon shot. The reporter has come adrift, both spatially and temporarily. The form of the moon trip that will reveal its meaning does not lie in the specific scenes and events that he is directed to observe, just as the trajectory of the rocket to the moon cannot be reduced to one single curve. The changing variations that affect a trajectory are so numerous that thousands must be simulated with the result that 'It is as if an artist drawing the curve of the arm had chosen in preference to one line, a thousand light strokes none in itself the outline, but taken all together a clear picture of an arm was present'.(129)

Because the entire moon shot, in effect, is a simulated reality, the novelist can only imaginatively engage with the project by constructing his own concepts of space and time. But this is achieved through a full recognition of how and why such forms have been destroyed by a society that has made such a moon shot possible. Aquarius discusses the technique of abstract painting in order to illustrate the profound discrepancy that exists between the apparent logic of this technological achievement and the confused disorder of its inner detail. He prefaces this discussion, however, with a general description of the far side of the moon, drawn from the photographs available. The longer Aquarius looks, the more frozen the landscape becomes, and so, the more meaningless. Like the rock in the centre of Magritte's room, like the single hypothesised trajectory, the 'wind-twisted choppy sea had been frozen on the instant to stone'(244) so that a recognisable sense of time and space is destroyed. Aquarius perceives that 'The instant of time suggested by the [Magritte] canvas was comparable to the mood of a landscape in the instant just before something awful is about to happen, or just after, one could not tell'.(108) The photography of the moon destroys all sense of scale. He concludes, however, with a fine analysis of Cézanne's technique. Aquarius considers it to be similar to the technology that makes the moon's landscape available to observers on earth. Like the photograph, a Cézanne painting destroys all distinguishing surface characteristics so that 'the orders of magnitude vanished . . .'.(245) Cézanne's vision is, to Aquarius, prophetic of the moon shot. The full force of Aquarius' pre-occupation with this opaque surface that lacks the magnitude that should belong to such a project, is expressed during the dinner given for Wernher von Braun, 'the *deus ex machina* of the big boosters!'(53) Aquarius is an invited guest, and he compares the effect that von Braun's presence has upon the gathering, with the American love of new and impressive experiences and places. He argues that the moon shot brings into focus an American instinct

> to keep the country innocent, keep it raw, keep it crude as a lout, have it indeed ready to govern the universe without an agreeable

culture to call its own—for then, virgin ore, steadfastly unde-
veloped in all the hinter-world of the national psyche, a single
idea could still electrify the land. Culture was insulation against a
single idea, and America was like a raw-boned lover gangling
into middle age, still looking for his mission.(58)

Aquarius analyses this wilful denial of historical process the night
before the launch, when he wanders among the many Americans
who have gathered in their tents, trailers and campers to watch the
event. In a curiously Whitmanesque statement, he summarises his
stance towards 'some portion of a million'(50) people electrified by
this single idea: 'Aquarius passes these sights like a stranger. He feels
in such surroundings a foreigner equally as much as he feels
American. It is his country, but he merely traverses it. His feet do
not take root'.(53) In his detailed listing of the many farflung areas
from which these people have come, Aquarius becomes omnipresent, appropriating the eyes which view the space ship as 'some
white stone Madonna in the mountains, welcoming footsore
travellers at dusk'.(49) But as Aquarius shifts his voice to become a
hypothetical NASA executive, the religious awe loses its primitive
connotations and becomes a manipulated spectacle utilising the
publicity afforded movie premières and Rockettes in Radio City. It
is the difference between the humble innocence of spiritual awe and
the raw and loutish innocence of simple, momentary sensation.
Then Aquarius becomes a Southern mill-worker, with an understanding of machines and a longing to be Neil Armstrong. The
loutishness is given an energy, an awe that gives it a momentary
dignity. The worker's wife, on the other hand, is too old to feel this
glorious but transient elation. They each reflect the best and worst
of the event.

Aquarius again develops opposing viewpoints when he temporarily leaves his assignment in order to visit wealthy European
friends, whose home provides a cultural island in Houston. One of
the guests, a black professor, engages Aquarius' attention during
most of the evening. Like himself, the professor 'lived half in the
world of numbers, and half in the wrappings of the [extrasensory]
aura'.(112) Yet in their discussion, Aquarius, who is long familiar
with the issues that must alienate this man from any WASP
technological achievement, maintains a distinct distance. Never
having 'been invited to enter this Black man's vision', he speculates
upon the professor's degree of militancy, he impartially observes

'that the fundamental notion of Black superiority might be incorrect' and then finally admits with simple satisfaction 'It was just that Aquarius was White and the other Black—so Aquarius could not conceal altogether his pleasure in the feat'.(111–12) It is only alone at night with his insomnia that Aquarius gradually feels the black professor's sense of angry alienation. He quotes a remark made by the professor which provides a moral footnote to his own thought at the dinner for von Braun: ' "Technology begins when men are ready to believe that the sins of the fathers are not visited on the sons" '.(113) In his developing reflections upon this notion, Aquarius gradually embodies this social and moral vacuum. He suffers from anaesthesia, he has no sense of the future. His previous belief in the counter-revolution of the hipster is replaced by a vision of society divided into rational and irrational camps, frozen into impotence.

Returning to his ego in the ironically titled final section, 'The Age of Aquarius', he engages in a maudlin diatribe against 'his people . . . an unholy stew of fanatics, far-outs, and fucked-outs where even the loved were intolerable at their worst, an army of outrageously spoiled children who cooked with piss and vomit . . .'.(357) There is no technique which Aquarius can employ, no issue which he can stress, to distance himself. It is a self-indulgent, sentimental show of subjectivity and it is intended to be so, because an enraged final question has already been answered. 'Who among all the people he knew well had the remotest say on the quality of these lunar expeditions . . .'.(ibid) No-one, of course, but Aquarius.

Throughout his narrative, Aquarius has considered the quality of space which is being invaded and the nature of the target itself: the moon. His inclination, which is to preserve their mystery, their possible hostility, is countered by NASA's assumption that they are blandly benign. The nature of the moon as an objective, scientific fact is not here at issue; it is 'the shot to the moon' which is 'a mirror to our condition—most terrifying mirror: one looked into it and saw intimations of a final disease'.(313) Of itself, with its pitted, twisted landscape, it reveals nothing. But having been conquered with a complete absence of visible emotion, it is the earth which has been transformed. Armstrong, on the moon, stares at the earth through the telescope and, 'Like the eye of a victim just murdered, the earth stared back at him'.(335) Like the moon, the vacuum of space is, in itself, of no consequence. The fact that it has been invaded reflects a mental and topographical emptiness. America is 'An empty country filled with wonders'(84) instead of the virgin land which Aquarius evokes on the dawn of the launch. His description of the land which existed in a time before abandoned launch towers, grain elevators, and railroad tracks avoids the use of tired, nostalgic epithets by simply suggesting in a single image a sensual, fertile landscape, 'an all but empty continent with lavender and orange in the rocks, pink in the sky, an aura of blue in the deep green of the forests . . . '.(68) The empty country here is not a vessel to be filled with wonders: its emptiness is a source of wonder.

All these reflections have a consequence which, to Aquarius, is anathema. To disregard the temporal and spatial dimensions is to believe that one has delivered oneself from mortality. Aquarius begins and ends with contrasting views on death. The mark of integrity to Hemingway and to Mailer, his lifelong admirer, is a recognition of the constant threat of death, and it is the news of Hemingway's suicide that opens the book, prefaced by that novelist's words: 'Now sleeps he with that old whore death . . . Do thee take this old whore death for thy lawful wedded wife?'(3) The book's penultimate section begins with a verse from Revelation, which indicates the price paid for ignoring that old whore: 'And in those days, men will seek death and will not find it; they will long to die and death will fly from them.'(374) In order to reinstate death, time and space which are the recognisable dimensions that have been so alarmingly disregarded, Aquarius introduces the concept of dread, which he attributes to Hemingway, but which Mailer has earlier developed in his own work.

In an article, included in *Cannibals and Christians* and entitled 'The Fear of God', Mailer argues that this is a necessary terror that originates from an awareness within the individual as to the constant precariousness of his 'courage, compassion, art, tenderness, skill, stamina and imagination . . .'.(420) This fear, which Mailer calls dread, has been ignored through the insulation of the senses, by modern drugs, by a society that is antisupernatural. Despite this familiarly generalised attack, Mailer's concern in the essay seems to be largely with the precariousness of the writer's creative imagination, which 'must struggle to carry this [noble] conception of Being out into the dark emptiness of the universe, there to war against other more malignant conceptions of Being . . . '.(ibid) In *St George and the Godfather*, however, Mailer clearly feels that the absence of dread is the source of a social malaise personified by

Richard Nixon. One of Aquarius' sinister parodies of Nixon's maxims states 'There is only one freedom looked for by the American voter who votes for Nixon—it is freedom from dread'.(217) But, as the opening chapter of *A Fire on the Moon* stresses, it is an impossible freedom: 'Dread was loose. The giant had not paid his dues, and something awful was in the air. Technology would fill the pause. Into the silences static would enter. It was conceivable that man was no longer ready to share the dread of the Lord.'(3–4) It is in the context of this initial enigmatic warning that Aquarius' notions on the psychology of machines can be considered. To believe that nothing is beyond the control or understanding of man is to reduce him to a machine. To realise that nothing is finally knowable or predictable in science is to restore man and his natural world to a moral balance that is suggestively Thoreauvian. Throughout his narrative, Aquarius provides numerous illustrations of inexplicable mechanical perversities in space flight.

Yet the concept of dread functions primarily, in *A Fire on the Moon*, as a metaphor by which Aquarius, the invisible novelist, shapes the hidden but purposeful dimensions of the moon trip. His initial insistence upon his loss of ego prefaces his discussion of 'the inner space of the dream'(127) which introduces 'The Psychology of Machines'. The ideas draw heavily upon Mailer's earlier essay 'Some Dirt in the Talk', in his location of an egotistical navigator in the unconscious. But to this navigator, assessing and projecting the individual's experience, Mailer substitutes the novelist in *A Fire on the Moon* for the actor in 'Some Dirt in the Talk'. The novelist records, gives a discernible form to inchoate insights based on the external world, although it is within the dream that the navigator discovers most. Because of the suggestion 'of a reality subtly beneath reality' which is 'more exciting, more threatening, more demanding and more rewarding than the easier reality of the working day surface',(131) the dream is 'indeed a simulation chamber' where this alternative reality can only truly be apprehended and tested. Aquarius never defines this submerged reality; it exists in his narrative principally to offer an emotional dimension to the dread which he discovers at this subliminal level within himself. 'He was exploring the depths of his own ability to perceive crisis and react to it . . .'.(ibid) Aquarius then invites an analogy between his own unconscious and the moon trip, 'as if, indeed, the literal moon trip was a giant species of simulation to reveal some secret in the buried tendencies of our history'.(132) But here, the services of the novelist are inadequate: it *remains* an analogy. In order for the moon trip to be dependent for its meaning upon the personae of Aquarius, the performance of his novelist needs to be less concerned with grand extended similes and more with metaphors that are constructed upon a concern for detail. Aquarius is aware of this weakness. His need 'to believe in God and to believe in progress'(122) is a vital premise to his narrative, but Aquarius can only elaborate these notions at the expense of adding such general qualifications as 'it was somehow superior to see the astronauts and flight of Apollo 11 as the instrument of such celestial or satanic endeavours . . .' (123) or 'such remarks are large, they are grand, they roll off into the murk of metaphysical storm'.(132)

In his close observation of the information available to him, Aquarius as novelist makes an important distinction between fact and reality. Because the fact of the first astronauts on the moon can provide no sensual correlative for the earthbound observer, Aquarius refuses to accept its reality. From the moment that the ghostly pictures are transmitted from the moon, there is nothing 'to prove it had not conceivably been an event staged in a television studio . . .'.(106) He will accept as a fact any information that has proved its validity to the navigator of his unconscious. So Aquarius can decide that because the story in *Life* describing Armstrong's recurrent dream of levitation endorses his theories on 'the architecture and function and presence of the dream',(41) he can choose 'to believe the dream had occurred'.(39) As a result, 'Any notes toward a new psychology could take their departure from here, from this *fact*'.(41) Reality, on the other hand, always emanates from Aquarius' navigational unconscious.

Aquarius discovered he was happy. There was a man on the moon. There were two men on the moon. It was a new feeling, absolutely without focus for him. If he felt a faint graveling on the surface of this sentiment, a curdle of emotional skin which formed from his effort to advance heroes he could not find altogether admirable, still he knew he had been dislocated as profoundly as by the experience as the moment he learned in the fathers' waiting-room at the hospital that his first child had indeed and actually just been born. 'Well, think of that,' he said. What a new fact! Real as the presence of immanence and yet not located at all, not yet, not in the comfortable quarters one afforded for the true and real facts of the life of the brain.(92)

This reaction to the sparse information, ' "Houston, Tranquility Base here. The Eagle has landed" ',(ibid) allows a qualifying reticence to skim the surface of his happiness without letting it disturb the validity of his controlled euphoria. Reality is a profound dislocation, 'absolutely without focus for him' because it is, as yet, at odds with 'the life of the brain'. Similarly, the retrospective account of the same event in the 'Apollo' section of the narrative is without focus, because its reproduced factual accuracy, with Armstrong's insistence on the hospitality of the moon is 'about as deep in a real knowledge of public opinion as any thought the colored races of the world could be soothed by Muzak'.(331) Mailer returns again to that crucial image which expresses the necessary integration of selfhood in both an individual and social sense: the ascent of the magician or the ego from the dungeon of the unconscious to the tower of the brain.

These levels of reality in Aquarius are organised around the oppositional personae of reporter and detective or novelist, but they are also represented by the uneasy conjunction of physics and engineering which is ultimately the successfully functioning union of Saturn V and Apollo 11. The first two sections of *A Fire on the Moon* are organised around this distinction.

> Physics was a study of the order and courtliness and splendor and bewildering mystery of the rule of action in nature, a contemplation of its forces; engineering was immersion into the slippage coefficient of the adhesive applied to the nut which held the bolt of one ten-millionth of the total conception fleshed into a machine . . .(146)

Aquarius contemplates with dread the forces of Saturn V in the 'Aquarius' section, while he becomes the 'scientific artist'[4] in the 'Apollo' section in order to concentrate principally upon the magnificently complex 'brain' of the rocket: Apollo 11. Saturn V and Apollo 11 can only perform as a functioning unit because 'the force of fire and the transmission of thought [which have] been harnessed into machines which sat within other machines' are 'two of the most perilous activities for primitive man'.(139) In order for Aquarius to restore the primitive awe that this controlled conjunction should properly command, he commences with a contemplation of Saturn V which successfully becomes a component of Aquarius' unconscious.

After wearily confronting the controlled public relations at Manned Spacecraft Centre, Aquarius begins his third chapter at Cape Kennedy where the rockets are constructed. His frustration at MSC is principally caused by the lack of tangible scale that is equal to the magnitude of the enterprise. This is rectified at the Cape. While MSC is a brain, Cape Kennedy is the body with 'the bones and muscles of a Colossus'.(43) So far, Aquarius' imagery deliberately stresses the brute force of these dimensions, which is confirmed by the gross external ugliness of the Vehicle Assembly Building. As he moves inside, however, his imagery gradually establishes a scale of another order. Initially, the space is superior to the UN Building, the Statue of Liberty. But just as Aquarius moves from without to within in order to discover beauty instead of ugliness, his imagery turns from the familiarly tangible American monuments to a rapid succession of images that indicate his bewildered respect and awe. Aquarius is physically situated at the top of the building where the light is dim yet translucent. At this height, he searches for a sense of familiarity, but fails because the experience is one of pure sensation.

. . . you could have been up in the rigging of a bridge built beneath the dome of some partially constructed and enormous subterranean city, or you could have been standing on the scaffolding of an unfinished but monumental cathedral, beautiful in this dim light, this smoky concatenation of structure upon structure, of breadths and vertigos and volumes of open space beneath the ceiling, tantalizing views of immense rockets hidden by their clusters of work platforms. One did not always know whether one was on a floor, a platform, a bridge, a fixed or impermanent part of this huge shifting ironwork of girders and suspended walkways. It was like being in the back of the stage at an opera house, the view as complex, yet the ceiling was visible from the floor and the ceiling was more than fifty stories up since above the rockets were yet some massive traveling overhead cranes. To look down from the upper stages of the rocket, or from the highest level where the crew would sit, was to open oneself to a study of the dimensions of one's fear of heights. Down, down, a long throw of the soul down, down again, still falling was the floor of the building, forty floors below. The breath came back into the chest from an abyss. And in the corner of the floor like a stamp on the edge of a large envelope was a roped-in square of several hundred tourists gawking up at the yellow cranes and the battleship-gray girders.(45)

Aquarius' declared failure to understand and control his sensual response, brilliantly synthesises the interior of the Vehicle Assembly Building and his own primitive unconscious. The simulated plunge from the dizzying height to the postage-stamp of tourists, with its perfectly modulated sense of scale, reconfirms the part of himself that Aquarius is forced to relinquish in order to experience this massive structure. His fear of heights, his compulsion to contemplate the bottom suggests a Poe-like perversity, confirmed by Aquarius' conclusions drawn from the experience.

For once, Aquarius must abandon his familiar refrain that questions *either* the sanity *or* insanity of the mission. The simulated plunge down to primitive dread, that literally traces the physical contours of the rocket's assembly, has suddenly rendered the question superfluous. Aquarius is down in 'those zones of silence' which contain 'a hint of that ancient dark beneath the hatch in the hold of the bow'(45) so that

> It was not that he suddenly decided to adopt the Space Program, or even approve it in part, it was just that he came to recognize that whatever was in store, a Leviathan was most certainly ready to ascend the heavens—whether for good or ill he might never know—but he was standing at least in the first cathedral of the age of technology, and he might as well recognize that the world would change, that the world *had* changed, even as he had thought to be pushing and shoving on it with *his* mighty ego.(46)

It is a crucial experience because the rest of the narrative depends upon the invisible, observing, witnessing Aquarius who can provide more than a 'ghost of a correlative'(30) to the projected moon trip. 'He was already in orbit himself, a simple fellow with a mind which idled agreeably, his mind indeed out in some weightless trip through the vacuum of a psychic space, for a mind without ego he was discovering is kin to a body without gravity'.(47)

This experience, however, has served to establish the physical scale of Saturn V. Before its momentous departure from earth, Aquarius turns to the fire which propels it. The force of fire is not only the literal means by which the rocket can levitate but the metaphorical force by which Aquarius can marry the technological achievement of the moon trip to the primitive sense of awe which it should command. In 'The Fear of God' Mailer argues that 'to primitive man fire was of course always a miracle, a dangerous miracle . . . he approached fire with profound respect . . .'(422) In *A Fire on the Moon*, Aquarius again insists that 'Savages had looked at fire and knew. God was in the wood of trees and in the core of everything which burned . . .'(136) Despite the angry interjections of the dissatisfied reporter in the hours and minutes leading up to blast-off, at the final moment 'Aquarius never had to worry again about whether the experience would be appropriate to his measure'.(81)

Just as the earthbound Aquarius is moved to primitive awe at the sight of Saturn V's levitation, he creates a similarly primeval fear in the release of a fire on the moon. Aquarius wades ironically through the vital statistics of astronauts and their attenuated technological jargon and, by means of his metaphor of the dream, reaches that moment on the moon when he can occupy without qualification the collective unconscious of Armstrong and Aldrin. Aquarius gives an informed factual account of the mechanism which is intended to take the Lem off the moon, before confronting the unconscious fear that this moment must provoke. The motor of the Lem has never previously been fired in a moon vacuum. With the astronauts, he waits for the predetermined moment to test the levitation of their vehicle, and re-engages with respect the primitive fears that had all but disappeared beneath their parody, on earth, of the conventional in their public manner. Confronted with the possibility of death, they are happy and afraid, scourged and exalted, but simultaneously 'in a cave of chilly isolation, happy, numb, and full of a fear of dreams . . .'(338) The moon has provided a context in which earthbound frozen oppositions have come together through Aquarius, the psychic astronaut.

As a result of this fruitful synthesis, the earth is transformed. Aquarius now pictures it as an 'eye to look at [the returning astronauts] in curious welcome as they return'.(350) Armstrong, Aldrin and Collins have become the heroes their conventional public manner was so reluctant to acknowledge before the journey. Aquarius therefore rediscovers in the earth they return to, the liquid proliferation of colour that he had mourned as forever gone, lost in some past time when the country was once virgin. It is virgin again.

Blue she will gleam and brown and gray and silver and rose and

red. Her clouds will cover her like curls of white hair, her clouds
will turn dark as smoky pearls and the lavender of orchid, her
clouds will be brown and green like marsh grass wet by the sea,
and the sea will appear beneath like pools of water in the marsh
grass.(350)

The sheer beauty of this description conclusively establishes a causal
connection between the virgin space upon and above the earth that
Aquarius had formerly searched for without success.

   With the return of the astronauts to earth, Aquarius resumes his
narrative as the earthbound observer. He is once again the
dislocated writer locked within his closely circumscribed ego. The
ultimate meaning of the moon trip eludes him. It is only when he
leaves Provincetown, armchair and wife and returns again to
Houston that Aquarius can move away from his private life, his
predominantly literal vision. The transition from the literal to the
metaphorical, from Aquarius' ego to his senses, enables him to
discover a psychic space upon which literal outer space depends.
The momentous return to his senses takes place in front of the moon
rock situated behind the same wall of glass that separated Aquarius
the reporter from the astronauts. As he looks at the moon rock with
his mind finally freed from the literal yet elusive dimensions of outer
space, he is able 'to comprehend the world once again as [a poet],
comprehend it as savages who knew that if the universe was a lock,
its key was a metaphor rather than measure'.(380)

   Mailer's books on the 1968 and 1972 National Conventions and
on the moon landing in 1969 are all based on the conviction that no
matter how recalcitrant the subject may be, there is 'something in
the shape of things' that respects 'any human who would force an
impossible solution up out of the soup, as if the soup itself were
sympathetic to the effort'.[5] *Miami and the Siege of Chicago, St George
and the Godfather* and *A Fire on the Moon* bear out the validity of this
statement. Yet the notion of forcing 'an impossible solution' suggests
the difficulties that Mailer would confront in the years to come.

5 'Faceless broads' and 'angels of sex'

Since 1972, Mailer seems to have been caught in a dilemma which he had predicted in several metaphors throughout his career. They all stress the notion of the artistic impulse as a limited natural resource of the writer. As a result Mailer has maintained a steady hatred of wasteful activity, which is especially apparent in his sexual metaphors. His aversion from contraception and masturbation, and his insistence upon the causal connection between orgasm and conception, indicate in his fiction, essays and polemical discussion, the respect, even awe, with which he regards his literary creativity. It is for this reason that Mailer discovers the immanence of death in the talent of Hemingway, Marilyn Monroe and himself. If Hemingway and Monroe literally died by their own hands, Mailer has had to defend his talents against something much more frightening. In 'The Metaphysics of the Belly' he graphically describes the dwarf within the self who wants to kill the magnificent senses of the artist.(310)[1] As Mailer's career gathered momentum, the meaning of these metaphors grew clearer in his writing. The senses are magnificent when they are shaped and given an interpretive authority by the personae that control the form of the narrative. They successfully hold at bay the fallible, messy, shapeless self that is at the mercy of the world. But there is a constant, underlying fear, which erupts in *The Prisoner of Sex* (1972), that this formless identity will suddenly take control and finally destroy his talent. Mailer's life will no longer be the life of the nation because his magnificent and fallible selves will cease to find a metaphorical synthesis in his writing.

This imbalance is apparent in the opening pages of *The Prisoner of Sex*, as the writer's public and private lives clash with his literary activity, which is situated in between these lives on a precarious no-mans-land. The possibility of receiving the Nobel Prize is juxtaposed with the failure of Mailer's fourth marriage, which provokes the sad reflection that fame has lost its meaning, since there is no sense of mission in the writer's current activities. When Mailer performs erratically on stage in *The Armies of the Night*, the account transforms a spontaneous and what was to become notorious exhibition into the purposeful act of a famous man. But, as the Prisoner sadly remarks, 'Fame, unless one had a mission, was equal to the taste of aspirin in one's death . . .'[2] and there is patently no mission in the writer's current activities—'For his battered not-so-firm ego was obliged to be installed in Provincetown through a long winter to go through the double haul of writing a book about the first landing on the moon while remaking himself out of the loss of a fourth wife'.(9) If this reference to Mailer's marital breakup is compared to Aquarius' earlier discussion of their growing estrangement, then the nature of his dilemma becomes clearer. In *A Fire on the Moon*, his wife is both an image that illustrates the earthly reverberations of the moon landing and a literal reality for the earthbound private man. While their quarrels have a long domestic history, there is also a lunar history to their relationship that Aquarius, after his assignment, can justifiably superimpose. As he develops his lunar metaphors, his wife, their marriage and the moon's phases synthesise, so that even a woman screaming at her husband becomes an awesome inevitability. In *The Prisoner of Sex*, however, Mailer's narrator can offer no meaning, beyond its prosaic literalness, to his private life. It is not a comparative point of reference, it does not carry symbolic connotations; it is simply a comfortable antidote to his recent emotional and creative lacerations. His ego, his reputation is resident in New York, beyond his immediate concern or control.

It is because the narrator of *The Prisoner of Sex* is safeguarding a self and a lifestyle which bears no relevance to his literary style, that the interpretive criteria of his book are so confused. He has given meaning to sex, but whether it is a literal or metaphorical meaning is never, at any stage, really established. This is because the Prisoner of sex has locked himself in and is therefore prevented from making a dialectical contact with the Prizewinner, who possesses the literary ego which is under attack. Although the Prisoner ostensibly mounts a counter-attack against Kate Millett, he is unwittingly forced into a defensive impasse because he has conceded, in part, to her critical stance, which is that of a moral realist. Millett reveals her misunderstanding of Mailer's writing in her reliance upon conventionally defined literary genres: ' . . . the most fascinating

problem in dealing with his writing is to establish the connection
between his fiction and his other prose writings, for ideas one is
convinced are being satirized in the former are sure to appear with
straightforward personal endorsement in the latter.[3] She is unaware
that when Mailer (like Henry Miller) employs a sexual metaphor, it
does not bring into play the whole self. In its literary context, the
sexual metaphor is only indirectly concerned with the political
frame of reference that Millett defines as 'power-structured relationships, arrangements whereby one group of persons is controlled by another'.[4] Yet despite Mailer's attempt to establish a
narrator who, as Prisoner or Prizewinner, balances the 'polar
concepts to be regarded at opposite ends of his ego', (9) each persona
is mutually exclusive. Millett's attack is, ironically, justified by the
counter-attack.

As a Prisoner, he is a man with an old love performing the role of
the housewife. But while he is a prisoner, he cannot cast an eye
towards the oppressed minority groups in New York without
obliviously reducing that world to the domain of the domestic
cliché. Alternatively, when he resuscitates the Prizewinner in order
to confront Women's Liberation, the Prisoner is irrelevant.
Remembering his political candidacy and his constant respect for
the power of women, he is moving suddenly into a literary
dimension where women are the figurative recipients of his creative
phallus. As the aesthetic revolutionist, he is forced to withdraw
before the economic, cultural and sexual revolution of the militant
feminists, because, as he himself is quick to discern, the literal
fighting in the street may yet displace the disillusioned writer who
has 'lost that essential belief in himself which was critical to the idea
that one could improve the world . . .'(56) What is curious and yet
central to the failure of the book, is that the Prizewinner or 'PW' is
never the active novelist, despite the quoted extracts from his own
work, which include *An American Dream*.

In his examination of militant feminist tracts and theories of
planned sex the PW's figurative defence from a literal attack
justifies this kind of eloquent reaction:

> Although it goes against the grain . . . I might very well when it
> comes down to biology, back Millett against Mailer. It would, I
> know it, be as good as backing Lenin against Jefferson, and as a
> woman, one could be as much betrayed in the end as the
> proletariat was destroyed. But I see how, for one dizzy moment,

you can back your betrayer for the sake of a single insight . . . If
the truth were known, if the truth could be known, the womb is
without privilege, the cock is without privilege; the mysterious
power of the space within never existed, the ontological power of
the cock, the Unhappy Consciousness, never existed. Sexuality is
as empty as a Kate Millett could conceive . . . .[5]

The PW counters the statistical and medical data assembled to
discount the vaginal orgasm, with his own experience, which raises
the spectre of an active, experienced lover. But the metaphor is
suddenly reinstated, as the necessity of the penis to the female
orgasm (and conception) is 'the life of the aesthetic, man with his
penis, woman with her womb . . .'.(83) Finally, the vaginal orgasm
is saved, not by the legions of women who furnish the PW with
practical proof, but by 'a net of metaphor suspended from a
nonexistent string . . . '.(90)

Similarly the PW takes issue with Millett's contention that
' "Whatever the real differences may be, we are not likely to know
them until the sexes are treated differently, that is alike" ',(128) by
recalling Mailer's fear of totalitarianism which he conceives of as
undifferentiated mediocrity. Although he proclaims her argument
fallacious on the grounds that she has pushed 'past the argument
that sex was not so much in the organs as the mind . . .',(129) he
allows himself to be confined within her frame of reference. After
considering the question of sexual distinctiveness, using biological
evidence that returns sexuality to the organs, he retreats back to the
mind with the disclaimer, 'It was never advisable, when knowing
little of these matters, to elaborate any thesis upon them. Who was
more to be disrespected than the philosopher who built his system
upon scientific conclusions he could not evaluate'.(131) By also
suggesting that racial distinctions are analogous, the PW conceives
of sexuality as the whole self, like Linda Phelps, in her essay 'What Is
the Difference?' The PW then abruptly shifts the base of his
argument from scientific and social data to 'the metaphorical feel,
the metaphorical drift, if you will, of his own thought . . .'(132)
without indicating either the terms of his metaphor or why and how
it is in any way distinct from his previous discussion. If all embryos
are at first alike, the PW finds it reasonable[6] to assume 'That one
had to alienate oneself from nature to become a man, step out of
nature, be almost as if opposed to nature, be perhaps directly
opposed to nature, be perhaps even the instrument of some larger

force in that blind goat-kicking lust which would debase females, make all women cunts . . .'.(ibid) When he finally admits the probable fallacies of such theories, the PW is not a conflicting persona that deepens the ambiguity of the argument. Instead, the remark dislocates the Prisoner's contention that he finds the notion of similarity between men and women aesthetically nauseating.

When Mailer's narrator turns from defending himself to defending Henry Miller and D. H. Lawrence from Millett's attack, he is both eloquent and consistent because here, if only indirectly, Mailer the novelist glimmers through the confused personae. He unerringly discerns in Miller's bombastic and raucous sexuality the best of his own fictional metaphors, while Lawrence's sensitive romanticism takes on the hue of Mailer's grand but certain failure in *An American Dream*. As long ago as 1956, in his review of *Waiting for Godot*, Mailer insisted that the purpose of the artist was 'to accelerate historical time itself. The velocity of history is made by the rate of increase of human consciousness, *provided* that consciousness can express itself in action and so alter society'.(262) This is the nature of the Hip revolution as conceived of by Mailer which he reiterates in his retrospective tribute to Miller who, 'with his brain and his balls in the intimate and continuing dialogue of his daily life . . . followed the line of [his] sexual impulse without a backward look at what was moral, responsible, or remotely desirable for society . . . '.(103)

As a result, Miller, like Mailer, can write like 'A demon . . . about bad fucks with all the gusto he gives to good ones, no fuck is in vain—the air may prove most transcendent at the edge of the vomit, or if not, then the nausea it produces can give birth to an otherwise undiscovered project as the mind clears out of its vertigo.'(104) The transcendence to which Mailer refers is what Sergius O'Shaugnessy discovers in his encounters with Denise which lead to her first orgasm. It is the jewelled city that Rojack glimpses after he has murdered Deborah. 'Poor Henry. He has spent his literary life exploring the watershed of sex from that uncharted side which goes by the name of lust and it is an epic work for any man . . . '.(109) But in introducing the term lust into his discussion and then distinguishing it from love, Mailer quietly begins to transfer his argument from an aesthetic to a conventionally moral dimension. Lust, as he defines it, is the sexual metaphor that Mailer and his protagonists employ to define their selfhood. To cry out in defence of the female recipient of this force is to defend what is not there, since, as Denise, Deborah and Ruta can testify, 'it appropriates loyalties, generalizes characters, leaches character out . . .'. They are 'faceless characterless pullulating broads . . .'.(117) The distinction between lust and love is saved till the end of Mailer's discussion on Miller, when he advances his own argument against Miller's fiction.

> Miller is right, yet Ibsen's Nora is also right when she says, 'I have another duty, just as sacred . . . My duty to myself . . . I believe that before everything else I'm a human being—just as much as you are . . . or at any rate, I shall try to become one'. What have we not lost in his novels that there will be never a character like Nora to stand against his men?(123–4)

To move from faceless broads to a human being is the goal of Rojack, when he discovers that he loves Cherry. Although the gently expressive romanticism of his language finds an appropriate context in his lovemaking with her, she hardly justifies its momentousness. She appears silly, even stupid, in her initial conversation with Rojack and never corroborates his conviction that she is exquisite and unique. The potential salvation that Cherry is clearly meant to offer Rojack demonstrates an important limitation in *An American Dream*. Mailer cannot satisfactorily create a woman who is a character rather than an antagonistic force.

It is as if Mailer needs Lawrence in *The Prisoner of Sex* in order to explain both his own desire for a self-sufficient woman in his fiction and why he was unsuccessful in *An American Dream*. If Miller embodies the sheer bawdy energy of Mailer's creativity, then Lawrence indicates its precariousness, which is the primary condition of its existence. Mailer understands that Lawrence's singular insight into 'the sensibility of a female burning with tender love' stems from his 'passion to be masculine as no other writer, he reminds us of the beauty of desiring to be a man, for he was not much of a man himself . . .'.(151–2) It is this last clause that indicates the nature of Mailer's withdrawal from Lawrence's fiction. His sensitive discussion of Lawrence's innate homosexuality is a measure of his own artistic fear. If lust, to Lawrence, is 'meaningless fucking' which is 'the privilege of the healthy'(155) then Mailer must assert his privilege, which from the point of view of the healthy renders lust meaningful. While Rojack rejects, with fear, the homosexual advances which are buried in the inviting taunts of Shago Martin, he is then intended by Mailer to be ready for the riches of love that Cherry offers him. Overt homosexuality must always, however, involve 'meaningless fucking', because the woman is 'without the power to be female, one is fucked without a womb, that is to say without awe'.(172–3)

But despite the masterful and sensitive manner in which this discussion of Lawrence is conducted, Mailer is again confusedly wandering between figurative and literal terms of reference. He uses biographical facts in order to illuminate the preoccupations of Lawrence's fiction, while the criteria he employs to evaluate these preoccupations are taken from the figurative use of them in his own fiction. Mailer, as the PW, attempts to elucidate this confusion in the concluding section of his book. By quoting extracts from 'An Impolite Interview' with Paul Krassner in which he defends his views on masturbation, the Prisoner who yearns for 'an accommodation of the sexes'(125) and the Prizewinner, whose literary successes have always been based on the premise that ' "the eternal battle with woman sharpens our resistance, develops our strength, enlarges the scope of our cultural achievements" '(ibid) arrive at a 'reasonable point: that there was a confrontation between fucking and reality'.(190) Yet in moving sex from a description of the act to a declaration of metaphysical design, it is impossible to know whether the decision that 'there is design in the universe, that humans embody a particular intent . . . [that] there is some kind of destiny intended—at the least!—*intended* for us, and therefore human beings are not absurd, not totally absurd . . .'(ibid) is a momentous realisation for the Prisoner or the Prizewinner. It cannot be both. Although the issue is later elucidated, it simply serves to justify Richard Poirier's irritated observation that Mailer 'is preposterously talking not about the experience of sex in time, on Monday or Tuesday or Saturday, but about sex in space, in a cartoon, a Platonic bubble over the head of the unwary copulator'.[7] It is the Prisoner who discerns the meaning in sex, but the woman herself is still not present; she is reserved to the end, when Cherry is seized from her fictional context, not to support the case for the prisoner but for the Prizewinner who reflects 'what an agony for a man if work were meaningless: then all such rights were lost before a woman'.(228)

Mailer, however, is able to achieve a dynamic exchange between the reality of sex and its transcendent meaning in *Marilyn* (1973). This is because he is dealing with a woman who is sufficiently real to provide him with biographical facts, should he choose to use them, and yet who is enough of a self-created legend to make her sympathetic to any interpretation Mailer might choose to make of her life and career. His term 'A Novel Biography' is aptly chosen. Mailer names no personae in this study; neither is it necessary since they are suggested by the subject herself. The first chapter establishes the various roles of Monroe through the several points of view of the writer. He is immediately an anonymous viewer of her films who responds to a sexual invitation that is essentially a manufactured intimacy. Mailer later enlarges upon this pheno-menon. 'Marilyn had become a protagonist in the great American soap opera . . . she is a character out there in the national life, alive, expected, even encouraged, to change each week. The spirit of soap opera, like the spirit of American optimism, is renewal . . . '. (94–5) When he moves on to the fact of her suicide in his opening chapter, the soap opera optimism peels away to reveal 'our exaggerated and now all but defeated generation . . . '.(17) Mailer has shifted his point of view to that of the fellow-artist who has based his own work upon 'the notion that exceptional people . . . had a way of living with opposites in themselves that could only be called schizophrenic when it failed'.(19) He is therefore equipped to detect the ambi-guity which lies in her sexuality and her simultaneous detachment from it.

When Mailer examines this ambiguity more closely in the light of his own theories on acting, he is momentarily indistinguishable from his subject. Monroe forces him to consider the problematic nature of the biography because she cannot necessarily be comprehended by the facts of her life. But he then goes on to discuss the enigmatic relationship between reality and fantasy in the life of a talented actress, which Mailer considers Monroe to be. This is arguable in the case of Monroe on the screen, but is a valid premise in so far as Mailer takes her to illustrate his conviction that 'an actor lives with the lie as if it were truth. A false truth can offer more reality than the truth that was altered'.(18) Mailer occupies his subject, in so far as she is the actor who, like Mailer, possesses a precarious sense of selfhood. Yet he is simultaneously distanced from her by the source material on which he must, to some extent, rely.

In his discussion of acting, Mailer contrasts the shifting roles which the actor assumes, with the true self that he believes Monroe spent her life trying to discover. Mailer himself becomes a nostalgic romantic in order to bring her literal sexuality into the compass of his own life. He buys her favourite perfume, is repelled by the smell, but then wistfully reflects 'But he would never have a real clue to how it smelled on her skin. Not having known her was going to prove, he knew, a recurrent wound in the writing, analogous to the regret, let us say, of not having been alone and in love in Paris when one was young'.(19) He seeks to rectify this loss by remembering the real possibility of meeting Monroe through Arthur Miller. But the vain fantasy of stealing her from Miller is a *recognised* confusion of figurative and literal sexuality which belongs to both Monroe and Mailer. Monroe is imagined in her marriage to Miller, as speaking 'to each man as if he were all of male existence available to her'.(20) Mailer withdraws from his fantasy with the reflection that 'It was only a few marriages (which is to say a few failures) later that he could recognize how he would have done no better than Miller and probably have been damaged further in the process'.(ibid) Mailer concludes his opening chapter with two observations that reconfirm his dual commitment to Monroe. On the one hand, her displayed presence to the world is 'managed and directed and advanced its insufferably difficult way forward by a harsh and near to maniacal voice of the most inward, concealed and secretive desperation, since the failure of her project was insanity, or some further variety of doom'.(23) This is not only that dwarf against which Hemingway fought and lost, but the dread which Mailer discerns within himself. Then as he briskly draws back from these disturbing reflections, Mailer is suddenly the biographer, viewing Monroe with an eye that is simply curious to know what distinguishes her from 'a million dumb and dizzy broads . . .'.(ibid)

In his account of Monroe's life, Mailer constantly returns to the uneasy and finally self-destructive relationship between the sexual personae that Monroe employs as an actress and her true, real self. Like the PW in *The Prisoner of Sex*, Mailer sees the distinction between this figurative and literal sexuality as one between lust and love. His account of her early career, based on the evidence of her film *Ladies of the Chorus* and the news photographs, stresses her tough sexual display, which reaches a climax in *Gentlemen Prefer Blondes*. Mailer compares the younger Monroe to 'the most popular blonde in the most expensive brothel in Acapulco'(78) and provides a photograph which amply illustrates this image, even while he knows the look is manufactured. He wants to establish a correspondence between the persona and her elusive private life, but because the facts are absent, Mailer seizes the opportunity to shape Monroe as the characterless sexual image that is crucial to her creative talent. She is like the women in Henry Miller's fiction, who can offer a view of sex which is 'the power to find some sexual return in a phallus or vagina as well as in a mirror or a lens'. (76) Love is explicitly distinct from this sexuality, because her whorish vacancy is an 'expression which was ready to suggest sexual pleasure and love could be taken in separate doses, and with separate people'. (ibid) By this logic, Monroe must have probably 'had a sex life of some promiscuity in this period'(78) and as both a biographer and a novelist, Mailer carefully establishes the validity of these claims.

When he writes about her adolescence, he draws from the known facts of her upbringing an image of her sexuality which is 'already without character. So she gave off a skin-glow of sex while others her age were still cramped and passionate and private . . . She was a general of sex before she knew anything of sexual war'.(43) At the peak of her career in the early 1950s, this impersonal sexuality has become a powerful persona that is channelled into the anonymous lens of the camera. Yet she is unable to control the images that the publicity machine releases. Mailer's premise, based on his own career, is that because Monroe is unable to control objectively her creative development, she destroyed herself.

> What an obsession is identity! We search for it, because the private sensation when we are in our own identity is that we feel sincere as we speak, we feel *real*, and this little phenomenon of good feeling conceals an existential mystery as important to psychology as the *cogito ergo sum*—it is nothing less than that the emotional condition of feeling real is, for whatever reason, so far superior to the feeling of a void in oneself that it can become for protagonists like Marilyn a motivation more powerful than the instinct of sex, or the hunger for position or money . . .
>
> The next question must obviously inquire what fearful objects or monsters are to be encountered in such a void, but it is a question to postpone until the wings of death lay wet feathers across her face.(86)

It is clear that Mailer is using Monroe to illustrate the importance of feeling emotionally real, which is his criterion of sincerity. She becomes another Mailer protagonist who demonstrates the precariousness of selfhood.

Mailer's preoccupation with the relationship between Monroe's life and career directs him to place particular emphasis upon her marriages to Joe DiMaggio and Arthur Miller. These marriages clearly illustrate the two aspects in Monroe of sexuality that the PW confusedly tries to elucidate in Henry Miller and D. H. Lawrence. Mailer gives DiMaggio an attitude toward sex that is comparable to Henry Miller's fictional lust—'Sexual prowess is more revered than any athletic ability but a good straight right. It is precisely because women are strange and difficult, and not at all easy, that they are respected enormously as trophies'.(99) And with that image, Mailer has explained what part of Monroe is committed to DiMaggio. Because her sexuality in this relationship with DiMaggio is indistinguishable from the figurative invitation on the screen, Mailer discovers two examples of sexual transcendence at this stage in her career. The novelist defines the double Monroe as 'one hard and calculating computer of a cold and ambitious cunt . . . and that other tender animal, an angel, a doe at large in blonde and lovely human form . . . It is her transcendence of these opposites into a movie star that is her triumph . . . '.(97) The end result of this duality is the unspoken question '"Gentlemen: ask yourself what really I am, for I pretend to be sexual and that may be more interesting than sex itself"'.(106)

While DiMaggio's creativity is active, Arthur Miller's is found in the style of a writer whose idea of himself is 'immense' but whose drama has 'become first cramped, then wholly constipated . . .'.(143) It is this discrepancy which Mailer finds hard to forgive in Arthur Miller, but which leads him to describe Monroe in her marriage to Miller as a goddess. Throughout her relationship with DiMaggio, she has no identity, but with Miller she can build an identity that is literally sexual, that can call forth a role involving the whole woman, 'be Marilyn Monroe, the wife of Arthur Miller'.(167) But because Monroe comes to Miller when his writing is at a temporary standstill, he adores and idealises her. We are back to the women in Lawrence's fiction, yet the sexual confusion at this stage in Monroe's life is the plot of Mailer's narrative which the novelist-biographer implicity comprehends and controls. Miller cannot maintain the image of Monroe as an adored goddess, because he has a commitment to his own creative talent. This talent produces *The Misfits*, which pushes Monroe's career into new developments, but which conclusively destroys any objective control she might exercise over it. Her performance in *The Misfits* suggests that 'she is not so much a woman as a presence, not an

actor, but an essence . . .'. (151) It is the end result of a process by
which Monroe's transcendent sexuality has been destroyed by the
juxtaposition of a marriage like 'the relation of cellmates who have
learned over the years to detest each other into the pit of each
intimate flaw' and a role which Miller must create for Monroe
which extols the 'beauty of her soul'.(193) Mailer's account of the
filming of *The Misfits* captures the pain of her death which he admits
has slipped away from the details that he constructs out of her dying.
Like *The Prisoner of Sex*, *Marilyn* is as much about the price that
Mailer himself has had to pay for his creative talents. Yet *Marilyn*
imposes the discipline of objectivity upon him by virtue of the
subject matter.

Despite the unmistakable achievement of *Marilyn*, however, it
suggests the growing uncertainty with which Mailer employs his
literary personae. His intermittent references to the Coquelin and
Stanislavsky schools of acting illustrate his uncertainty. Coquelin
suggests to Mailer that mode of acting which is completely divorced
from the person performing a role; a technique that, on more than
one occasion in his narrative, is eminently suited to Monroe 'who
has become an actor to avoid that hungry hole of the mind which
asks, "Who am I?" '(193) Yet the Method school of acting founded
by Stanislavsky also answers her need. Lacking any identity, she can
become what she is playing, be possessed by her roles. Mailer
appears, at several points in his narrative, to favour one and then the
other.

Similarly, in his recent anthology of Henry Miller's writing, *Genius and Lust*, Mailer's discussion of the relationship between an
individual's acted and real identity is ambiguous. He points out that
the woman with whom Miller was obsessed for thirty-six years was a
consummate actress. To June, life was a series of shifting scenarios
that were part of a created life. June can guide Miller into a similar
intuition about his own lack of identity, which is the core of his
creative talent. It leads him to that existential revolt in his writing,
already stressed by Mailer in *The Prisoner of Sex*.

> He has never looked back in moral guilt because whatever act he
> committed yesterday, and it could have been atrocious, heinous,
> or incommensurately disloyal to what he thought he believed or
> loved, it hardly mattered. He could look yesterday's act in the eye
> because the man who did it was no longer himself. In the act of
> doing it, he became another man, free to go in another direction.[8]

June, however, is not only an inspiration to the literary talent of Miller, as Monroe was to Mailer; she also obsesses Miller as a real woman with whom he was once hopelessly and faithfully in love. He is therefore forced endlessly to pursue her changing roles in his fiction in search of her non-existent reality. The result, according to Mailer, is that in the 1600 pages of *The Rosy Crucifixion* Miller 'never succeeds, never quite, in making her real to us, as novelistically real as Anna Karenina or Emma Bovary. She hovers in that space between the actual and the fictional where everything is just out of focus'.(181)

Mailer draws an important distinction in the nature of June's influence upon the literary career of Miller. She initially prompts him, in *The Tropic of Cancer*, to be an elusive character by means of his extraordinary stylistic versatility. But in *The Rosy Crucifixion*, June forces Miller to embark upon a literal search for her identity and, by implication, his own. In the light of *The Prisoner of Sex* and *Marilyn*, it is apparent that Mailer is again anxiously confronting his own preoccupations. A literary talent is only safe if the several styles of the protagonist are absolutely distinct from his creator. The fate of Monroe clearly rests upon a dangerous confusion of this nature, where her figurative roles are finally inseparable from her real self. In *Genius and Lust*, Mailer embarks upon a discussion of the nature of art, taking as his criterion the separation of the artist's ego from his literal self. Although Miller's life always impinges upon his writing, the description of his experiences in *The Tropic of Cancer* is always a literary act because he 'creates art as a species of spin-off from the more fundamental endeavor which is to maintain some kind of relation between his mind and the theatre beyond his mind which pretended to call itself reality'.(84) This all-important distinction between the artist's imaginative rendering of reality and literal reality which, according to Mailer, the memory of June was to undermine in Miller's writing, restates Mailer's dichotomy between lust and love. As in *Marilyn*, Mailer can legitimately invoke biographical information because it is central to his thesis which explains the demise of Miller's talent. Miller himself recounts in *The World of Sex* his longing for an idealised blonde, blue-eyed girl that he has seen, even while he is embarked upon an affair with an older woman. Mailer points out that while Miller was a sexual prodigy, the untouchable girl represents an ideal of love that Miller will never realise, but which he will never cease to pine for.

Mailer insists that for Miller (and by implication, for himself) lustful sex is a metaphorical force which the artist can wield in order to create his protagonist and the world in which he moves. So the sexual encounters in *The Tropic of Cancer* can metaphorically create the social milieu of Paris. Mailer singles out for an illustration, 'Miller and Van Norden . . . exhaustedly fucking a worn-out whore like men standing up in the trenches'.(187) But Miller's literary obsession with June in *The Rosy Crucifixion* does not 'short-circuit society'(ibid) because his sexual adventures are no longer figurative. The relationship between Miller and June is described by Mailer as that between two narcissists. Instead of the self being artistically defined by the momentary conjunction of the individual and his context, Miller seeks a literal control over external events in order to maintain a love that cannot bear change. *The Rosy Crucifixion*, to Mailer, is therefore a circular lament for the reality of June by an ego that is unmediated by the artistic imagination.

Yet Mailer cannot bring himself to reject the possibility of a true fictional heroine. He cannot relinquish the notion that June necessarily started Miller upon his literary career. If a woman is an individual, separate from the artist but equal to the force of his literary ambition, she can, according to Mailer, propel him into a relationship where the literal fact of their love can provide him with the fuel to embark upon sexual activities which convert his phallus into a literary weapon, that slays 'social artifice . . . and hypocrisy, and all the cancers of bourgeois suffocation'.(180) But if a woman is so powerful, her literal reality suffuses and finally undermines the activity of the artist. 'Indeed, part of Miller's continuing literary obsession with his second wife for close to thirty more years is due to the variety of her roles. Each offered a new role for Miller to play opposite'.(189) Mailer's own constant references to his wives in his writing since *The Armies of the Night* testifies to the importance of this issue to his own creativity. But the unsteadiness of his achievement in this respect indicates a lack of control over the process by which his actual sexual partners are transformed into the figurative dimension of his writing.

Gradually, the power and significance of Mailer's personae have diminished, the tactics they employ no longer seem so exciting or dangerous. It seems as if Mailer can no longer find a frame of reference that is provocative to his talents. He had replaced his earlier protagonists with fictional versions of himself in order that social and literary realms could be synthesised. The result, as he points out in *The Armies of the Night*, is that 'the clue to discovery was not in the substance of one's idea, but in what was learned from the style of one's attack'.(36) In the absence of firmly expressed ideological convictions, Mailer became dependent upon events that would suggest and invite a style of attack that was conducive to his creative imagination. But in recent years, his response to social and political issues has been one of disillusioned preoccupation, while Mailer's grand idea of the novel seems, as yet, to be as elusive a goal as it has always been.

Mailer's self-conscious tactics, however, have and will always operate best under a sense of threat. Whenever he has risked and apparently lost most, he has produced his best works. He now needs to find a new and suitably dangerous force, whether it is literally or figuratively defined, against which he can pitch his creative process. That force could conceivably be the apparently irrepressible urge that constantly pushes Mailer into the public arena and out of a solitary and disciplined mode of writing. In *The Prisoner of Sex*, he ruefully observes that 'he had by now lost that essential belief in himself which was critical to the idea that one could improve the world (and knew he might not regain that belief until he had written the novel of his life and succeeded in passing judgement on himself—if indeed one could) . . .'(56) To take discussions of his own writing quite literally is misleading, but an observation like this does demonstrate a general awareness, on the part of Mailer, of the necessity for new literary fields into which he can write himself.

Notes

INTRODUCTION

1. Norman Mailer, *The Armies of the Night* (London: Penguin Books, 1970), p. 32. Subsequent references to this edition will appear in the text.
2. Norman Mailer, *Advertisements for Myself* (London: Panther Books, 1968), p. 181. This edition includes 'A Calculus At Heaven' (1944), 'The White Negro' (1957), 'The Time of Her Time' (1959), 'Hip, Hell, and the Navigator' (1958) which is an interview with Mailer by Richard G. Stern, 'The Man Who Studied Yoga' (1952), 'David Riesman Reconsidered' (1954) which is a review of Riesman's book *Individualism Reconsidered*, 'A Public Notice on *Waiting for Godot*' (1956) and 'From Surplus Value to The Mass-Media' (1959). Subsequent references to these pieces, as well as to Mailer's 'Advertisements', will be to this edition and will appear in the text.
3. Richard Poirier, *A World Elsewhere: The Place of Style in American Literature* (London: Chatto and Windus, 1967), p. 11.
4. Mailer uses the term 'history' in both a personal and collective sense. This point is elucidated below in this chapter.
5. Norman Mailer, *The Naked and the Dead* (London: Panther Books, 1957), p. 153. Subsequent references to this edition will appear in the text.
6. Norman Mailer, *Cannibals and Christians* (London: Sphere Books, 1969), p. 101. This edition includes 'In the Red Light: A History of the Republican Convention in 1964', 'A Speech at Berkeley on Vietnam Day' (1965), 'Some Children of the Goddess' (1963), 'The Art of Fiction: A *Paris Review* Interview' with Mailer by Steven Marcus (1964), 'The Metaphysics of the Belly' (1966), and 'The Political Economy of Time'. Subsequent references to these pieces will be to this edition and will appear in the text.
7. Ihab Hassan, *The Literature of Silence: Henry Miller and Samuel Beckett* (New York: Alfred A. Knopf, 1967), p. 7.
8. Ibid., p. 15.
9. Ibid., p. 8.
10. Ibid., p. 12.
11. Ibid., p. 13.
12. In Norman Mailer, *The Presidential Papers* (London: Penguin Books, 1968). This edition also includes 'An Evening with Jackie Kennedy, or, The Wild West of the East' (1962), 'An Impolite Interview' (1962) with Mailer by Paul Krassner and 'Ten Thousand Words a Minute' (1962). Subsequent references to these pieces will be to this edition and will appear in the text.
13. 'Fictional reporting' refers principally to *The Armies of the Night, Miami and the Siege of Chicago* (and later in 1970, *A Fire on the Moon* and in 1972, *St George and the Godfather*). These texts are the subjects of Chapters 7 and 8.

CHAPTER I 'THE PECULIAR MEGALOMANIA OF A YOUNG WRITER'

1. Diana Trilling, 'Norman Mailer', *Encounter*, 19 (November 1962), 45–56, reprinted under the title 'The Radical Moralism of Normal Mailer', in N. Balakian and C. Simmons (eds.), *The Creative Present: Notes on Contemporary American Fiction* (New York: Doubleday and Company, Inc., 1963), p. 154.
2. Tony Tanner, *City of Words* (London: Jonathan Cape, 1971), p. 351.
3. Diana Trilling, p. 153.
4. Norman Mailer, *Barbary Shore* (New York: Signet Books, 1951), p. 7. Subsequent references to this edition will appear in the text.
5. J. W. Aldridge, 'Foreword', to G. A. Panichas (ed.), *The Politics of Twentieth-Century Novelists* (New York: Hawthorn Books, Inc., 1971), p. xi.
6. Ibid.
7. Ibid., p. xiv.
8. Ibid., p. xv.
9. Ibid., p. xiv.
10. Norman Mailer, *The Deer Park* (London: Corgi Books, 1962), p. 118. Subsequent references to this edition will appear in the text.
11. Diana Trilling, op. cit., p. 163.
12. Ibid., p. 162.
13. From Walter Allen, *The Urgent West: An Introduction to the Idea of the United States* (London: John Baker, 1969), p. 113.
14. Leslie A. Fiedler, *An End to Innocence: Essays on Culture and Politics* (Boston: The Beacon Press, 1948), p. 154.
15. See below, p. 122.
16. In Norman Mailer, *Existential Errands* (Boston: Little, Brown and Company, 1972), pp. 179–80, under the title 'Up the Family Tree'. This edition also includes 'Some Dirt in the Talk' (1967) and 'An Imaginary Interview' (1967). Subsequent references to these pieces will be to this edition and will appear in the text.

CHAPTER 2 'THE EXISTENTIAL HERO' AND THE 'BITCH GODDESS'

1. Brock Brower, 'Always the Challenger', *Life*, 18 October 1965, p. 49.
2. Ibid.
3. James Guetti, *The Limits of Metaphor* (New York: Cornell University Press, 1969), p. 178.
4. Norman Mailer, *Deaths for the Ladies (and other disasters)* (New York: Signet Books, 1971), reprinted in *Cannibals and Christians*, p. 194. *Deaths for the Ladies (and other disasters)* is not paginated.
5. Richard Poirier, *The Aesthetics of Contemporary American Radicalism* (Leicester: Leicester University Press, 1972), p. 13.
6. Ibid., p. 12.
7. Ibid., p. 23.
8. Ihab Hassan, 'Beyond a Theory of Literature: Intimations of Apocalypse?', *Comparative Literature Studies*, 1, No. 4 (1964), 261–71.
9. James Guetti, op. cit., p. 6.
10. Norman Mailer, *An American Dream* (London: André Deutsch, 1965) p. 45.

Subsequent references to this edition will appear in the text.

11. Northrop Frye, *Anatomy of Criticism: Four Essays* (Princeton: Princeton University Press, 1957), p. 223.
12. Ibid., p. 224.
13. Tony Tanner, *City of Words*, p. 363.

CHAPTER 3 'A FRUSTRATED ACTOR'

1. Norman Mailer, *The Deer Park: A Play* (London: Weidenfeld and Nicolson, 1970).
2. Norman Mailer, *Maidstone: A Mystery* (New York: Signet Books, 1971), p. 161. Subsequent references to this edition will appear in the text.
3. Norman Mailer, *Deaths for the Ladies (and other disasters)*, op. cit.
4. Norman Mailer, *Why Are We in Vietnam?* (London: Panther Books, 1970), p. 22. Subsequent references to this edition will appear in the text.
5. Marshall McLuhan, *Understanding Media: The Extensions of Man* (London: Sphere Books, 1967), p. 68.
6. Ibid., p. 71.
7. Norman Mailer, *St George and the Godfather* (New York: Signet Books, 1972), p. 218. Subsequent references to this edition will appear in the text.
8. Mailer is, however, working upon a long novel, which he had hoped to complete in 1979. For a brief account of this work in progress, see Herbert Mitgang, 'Mailer Takes on the Heavyweight Novel', *The New York Times*, 10 December 1976, p. 24. Nothing has so far emerged.
9. James Baldwin, 'The Black Boy Looks at the White Boy', *Esquire*, 55 (May 1961) 102–6, reprinted in R. F. Lucid (ed.), *Norman Mailer: The Man and His Work* (Boston, Toronto: Little, Brown and Company, 1971), p. 235.
10. Peter Manso, 'An Interview with Norman Mailer', in Peter Manso (ed.), *Running Against The Machine* (New York: Doubleday and Company, Inc., 1969), p. 4.
11. George A. Panichas, 'The Writer and Society: Some Reflections', in George A. Panichas (ed.), *The Politics of Twentieth Century Novelists* (New York: Hawthorn Books, Inc., 1971) p. xxxix.
12. Ibid.
13. Christopher Lasch, *The New Radicalism in America 1889–1963* (New York: Alfred A. Knopf, 1965), p. 333.
14. Ibid., p. 334.
15. Norman Mailer, 'A Transit to Narcissus—*Last Tango in Paris* directed by Bernardo Bertolucci', *The New York Review of Books*, 17 May 1973, p. 7.
16. Ibid.
17. Ibid., p. 9.
18. Ibid., p. 8.
19. Ibid., p. 9.

CHAPTER 4 THE NOVELIST VERSUS THE REPORTER

1. Norman Mailer, *Miami and the Siege of Chicago* (London: Penguin Books, 1969), p. 14. Subsequent references to this edition will appear in the text.

2. Gary Wills, 'St George and the Godfather', *The New York Times Book Review*, 15 October 1972, p. 1.
3. Norman Mailer, *A Fire on the Moon* (London: Weidenfeld and Nicolson, 1970), p. 122. Subsequent references to this edition will appear in the text.
4. A term first coined by Mailer in *Cannibals and Christians* p. 349.
5. Norman Mailer, *Marilyn* (London: Coronet Books, 1974), p. 19. Subsequent references to this edition will appear in the text.

CHAPTER 5 'FACELESS BROADS' AND 'ANGELS OF SEX'

1. See above p. 54.
2. Norman Mailer, *The Prisoner of Sex* (London: Weidenfeld and Nicolson, 1971), p. 8. Subsequent references to this edition will appear in the text.
3. Kate Millett, *Sexual Politics* (New York: Doubleday and Company, Inc., 1970), p. 328.
4. Ibid., p. 23.
5. Anita Van Vactor, from a letter to Richard Poirier, quoted by him in *The Aesthetics of Contemporary American Radicalism*, p. 14.
6. Reason, common sense and paranoia are equated more than once in order that Mailer's narrator can appear to be taking the militant ladies on their own logical terms while introducing his familiar demonology.
7. Richard Poirier, p. 13.
8. Norman Mailer, *Genius and Lust: A Journey Through the Major Writings of Henry Miller* (New York: Grove Press, Inc., 1976), pp. 183–4. Subsequent references to this edition will appear in the text.

Selected Bibliography

WORKS BY MAILER

The following references are to first editions.

The Naked and the Dead (New York: Holt, Rinehart and Winston, 1948).
Barbary Shore (New York: Holt, Rinehart and Winston, 1951).
The Deer Park (New York: G. P. Putnam's Sons, 1955).
'The White Negro' (San Francisco: City Lights Books, 1957). (Reprinted in *Advertisements for Myself*).
Advertisements for Myself

Deaths for the Ladies (and other disasters) (New York: G. P. Putnam's Sons, 1962).
The Presidential Papers (New York: G. P. Putnam's Sons, 1963).
An American Dream (New York: The Dial Press, 1965). (Originally published in *Esquire*, January to August 1964).
Cannibals and Christians (New York: The Dial Press, 1966).
The Bullfight: A Photographic Narrative with Text by Norman Mailer (New York: C.B.S. Legacy Books, distributed by the Macmillan Company, 1967). (Reprinted as 'Homage to El Loco' in *Existential Errands*).
The Deer Park: A Play (New York: The Dial Press, 1967).
The Short Fiction of Norman Mailer (New York: Dell Publishing Company, 1967).
Why Are We in Vietnam? (New York: G. P. Putnam's Sons, 1967).
Wild 90 (film) (1967).
Beyond the Law (film) Distributed by New Line Cinema (1968).
Miami and the Siege of Chicago (New York: New American Library, 1968).
The Armies of the Night (New York: New American Library, 1968).
The Idol and the Octopus (New York: Dell Publishing Company, 1968).

Maidstone (film) Distributed by New Line Cinema (1970).

A Fire on the Moon (Boston: Little, Brown and Company, 1970). (Published in America under the title *Of a Fire on the Moon*).

Maidstone: A Mystery (New York: New American Library, 1971).

On the Fight of the Century: King of the Hill (New York: New American Library, 1971).

The Long Patrol: 25 Years of Writing from the Work of Norman Mailer, edited and with an introduction by Robert F. Lucid (New York: World Publishing, 1971).

The Prisoner of Sex (Boston: Little, Brown and Company, 1971).

St George and the Godfather (New York: New American Library, 1972).

Existential Errands (Boston: Little, Brown and Company, 1972).

Marilyn (New York: Grosset and Dunlap, 1973).

The Faith of Graffiti, Text by Norman Mailer, design and art direction by Mervyn Kurlansky, photographs by Jon Naar. (New York: Praeger, 1974).

The Fight (Boston: Little, Brown and Company, 1975).

Genius and Lust: A Journey Through the Major Writings of Henry Miller (New York: Grove Press, Inc., 1976).

Some Honorable Men: Political Conventions 1960–1972 (Boston: Little, Brown and Company, 1976).

SOME UNCOLLECTED PIECES BY MAILER

'Talking of Violence', *Twentieth Century*, 173 (Winter 1964–65), 109–14.

'Mr Mailer Interviews Himself', *The New York Times Book Review* (17 September 1967), 4–5, 40.

Introduction to Charles Rembar, *The End of Obscenity* (New York: Bantam Books, 1969), v–ix.

'A Transit to Narcissus: *Last Tango in Paris* directed by Bernardo Bertolucci', *The New York Review of Books* (17 May 1973), 3–10.

'The Capote Perplex: An Open Letter from Norman Mailer', *Rolling Stone* (19 July 1973), 6.

'The Trial of the Warlock', *Playboy* (December 1976), 121–4, 126, 132, 232, 235–6, 240, 243–4, 246, 249–52, 254, 256.

'Of a Small and Modest Malignancy, Wicked and Bristling With Dots', *Esquire* (November 1977), 126–48.

CRITICAL MATERIAL

Books

Adams, Laura, *Norman Mailer: A Comprehensive Bibliography* (New York: Scarecrow, 1974).

Aldridge, John W., *After the Lost Generation* (London: Vision Press Limited, 1951).

Baldwin, James, *Nobody Knows My Name* (New York: Dial Press, 1961).

Bergonzi, Bernard, *The Situation of the Novel* (London: Macmillan Press, 1970).

Braudy, Leo, ed., *Norman Mailer: A Collection of Critical Essays* (New Jersey: Prentice-Hall, 1972).

Cleaver, Eldridge, *Soul On Ice* (London: Jonathan Cape, 1969).

Eisinger, Chester E., *Fiction of the Forties* (Chicago: University of Chicago Press, 1963).

Fiedler, Leslie A., *Waiting for the End: The American Literary Scene from Hemingway to Baldwin* (New York: Stein and Day, 1965).

Flaherty, Joe, *Managing Mailer* (New York: Coward McCann, Inc., 1969).

Jackson, Richard, *Norman Mailer* (Minneapolis: University of Minneapolis Press, 1968).

Geismar, Maxwell, *American Moderns: From Rebellion to Conformity* (New York: Hill and Wang, 1958).

Gelnius, Joseph, ed., *The Film Director as Superstar* (New York: Doubleday and Company, Inc., 1970).

Harper, Howard M., *Desperate Faith: A Study of Bellow, Salinger, Mailer, Baldwin and Updike* (Chapel Hill: The University of North Carolina Press, 1967).

Hassan, Ihab, *Radical Innocence: The Contemporary American Novel* (Princeton: Princeton University Press, 1961).

Howe, Irving, *A World More Attractive: A View of Modern Literature and Politics* (New York: Horizon Press, 1963).

Kaufmann, Donald L., *Norman Mailer: The Countdown (the first twenty years)* (Carbondale: Illinois University Press, 1970).

Kazin, Alfred, *Contemporaries* (London: Secker and Warburg, 1963).

Kazin, Alfred, *Bright Book of Life: American Novelists and Storytellers from Hemingway to Mailer* (London: Secker and Warburg, 1971).

Lasch, Christopher, *The New Radicalism in America 1889–1963* (New York: Alfred A. Knopf, 1965).

Leeds, Barry J., *The Structured Vision of Norman Mailer* (Leeds: Leeds University Press, 1967).

Lucid, Robert F., ed., *Norman Mailer: The Man and His Work* (Boston, Toronto: Little, Brown and Company, 1971).

Manso, Peter, ed., *Running Against the Machine* (New York: Doubleday and Company, Inc., 1969).

Millett, Kate, *Sexual Politics* (New York: Doubleday and Company, Inc., 1970).

Podhoretz, Norman, *Doings and Undoings* (New York: Farrar, Straus and Giroux, Inc., 1964).

Poirier, Richard, *The Performing Self: Compositions and Decompositions in the Language of Contemporary Life* (New York: Oxford University Press, 1971).

Poirier, Richard, *Mailer* (London: Fontana, 1972).

Poirier, Richard, *The Aesthetics of Contemporary American Radicalism* (Leicester: Leicester University Press, 1972).

Radford, Jean, *Norman Mailer: A Critical Study* (London: Macmillan Press, 1975).

Rideout, Walter B., *The Radical Novel in the United States, 1900–1954* (Cambridge: Harvard University Press, 1956).

Solotaroff, Robert, *Down Mailer's Way* (Carbondale: Illinois University Press, 1974).

Spatz, Jonas, *Hollywood in Fiction: Some Versions of the American Myth* (The Hague: Mouton and Company, 1969).

Tanner, Tony, *City of Words* (London: Jonathan Cape, 1971).

Trilling, Diana, *Claremont Essays* (New York: Harcourt, Brace and World, 1964).

Articles

Aldridge, John W., 'Victim and Analyst', *Commentary* (March 1966), 131–3.

Alvarez, Alfred, 'Norman X: *An American Dream*', *Spectator* (7 May 1965), 603.

Barnes, A., 'Norman Mailer: A Prisoner of Sex', *Massachusetts Review* 13 (Winter–Spring 1972), 269–74.

Bone, Robert A., 'Private Mailer Re-Enlists', *Dissent* (Autumn 1960), 3–10.

Brower, Brock, 'Always the Challenger', *Life* (18 October 1965), 46–57.

Bryant, Jerry H., 'The Last of the Social Protest Writers', *Arizona Quarterly*, 19 (Winter 1963), 314–25.

Busch, F., 'Whale as Shaggy Dog: Melville and "The Man Who Studied Yoga"', *Modern Fiction Studies*, 19 (Summer 1973), 193–206.

Chase, Richard, 'Novelist Going Places', *Commentary* (December 1955), 581–3.

Corrington, J. W., 'An American Dreamer', *Chicago Review*, 18 (Fall 1965), 58–66.

DeMott, B., 'Unprofessional Eye: Docket No. 15883', *American Scholar*, 30 (Spring 1961), 232–37.

Dickstein, Morris, 'A Trip to Inner and Outer Space' *The New York Times Book Review* (10 January 1971), 1, 42–3, 45.

Dupee, F. W., 'American Norman Mailer', *Commentary* (February 1960), 128–32.

Epstein, Joseph, 'Norman Mailer: The Literary Man's Cassius Clay', *New Republic* (17 April 1965), 42.

Ferris, Timothy, 'Reliable Source: Norman Mailer's Sex Change Operation', *Rolling Stone* (15 March 1973), 35.

Fiedler, Leslie A., 'Caliban or Hamlet: An American Paradox', *Encounter*, 25 (April 1966), 23–7.

Finholt, Richard D., '"Otherwise How Explain?" Norman Mailer's New Cosmology', *Modern Fiction Studies*, 17 (Autumn 1971), 375–86.

Geismar, Maxwell, Review of *The Naked and the Dead*, *Saturday Review*, 8 (January 1949), 35.

Gilman, Richard, 'Why Mailer Wants to be President', *New Republic* (8 February 1964), 17–20.

Glicksberg, Charles I., 'Norman Mailer: The Angry Young Novelist in America', *Wisconsin Studies in Contemporary Literature* (Winder 1960), 25–34.

Goldman, Lawrence, 'The Political Vision of Norman Mailer', *Studies On The Left*, 4 (Summer 1964), 129–41.

Hassan, Ihab, 'The Way Down and Out', *Virginia Quarterly Review*, 39 (Winter 1963), 81–93.

Hoffman, Frederick J., 'Norman Mailer and the Revolt of the Ego: Some Observations of Recent American Literature', *Wisconsin*

Studies in Contemporary Literature (Autumn 1961), 5–12.

Howe, Irving, 'Some Political Novels', *Nation* (16 June 1951), 568–9.

Hux, Samuel, 'Mailer's Dream of Violence', *Minnesota Review*, 8, No. 2 (1968), 152–7.

Kaufman, Donald L., 'The Long Happy Life of Norman Mailer', *Modern Fiction Studies*, 17 (Autumn 1971), 347–59.

Kazin, Alfred, 'The Trouble He's Seen', *The New York Times Book Review* (5 May 1968), 1–2, 26.

Kermode, Frank, 'Rammel', *New Statesman* (14 May 1965), 765–6.

Krim Seymour, 'An Open Letter to Norman Mailer', *Evergreen Review* (February 1967), 86–96.

Lennon, Michael J., 'Mailer's Sarcophagus: The Artist, The Media, and The "Wad"' *Modern Fiction Studies*, 23, No. 2 (Summer 1977), 179–87.

Leonard, John, 'Happy Birthday, Norman Mailer! The Last Word', *The New York Times Book Review* (18 February 1972), 30.

Lodge, David, 'Novelist at the Crossroads', *Critical Quarterly* (Summer 1969), 105–32.

Lucid, Robert F., 'Three Public Performances! Fitzgerald, Hemingway, Mailer', *American Scholar*, 43 (Summer 1974), 447–66.

MacDonald, Dwight, 'Art, Life and Violence', *Commentary* (June 1962), 169–72.

Meridith, Robert, 'The 45-Second Piss: A Left Critique of Norman Mailer and *The Armies of the Night*', *Modern Fiction Studies* 17 (Autumn 1971), 433–49.

Merrill, Robert, 'Norman Mailer's Early Nonfiction: The Art of Self-Revelation', *Western Humanities Review*, 28, No. 1 (Winter 1974), 1–12.

Mitgang, Herbert, 'Mailer Takes on the Heavyweight Novel', *The New York Times* (10 December 1976), 24.

Mudrick, M., 'Mailer and Styron: Guests of the Establishment', *The Hudson Review* 17 (Autumn 1971), 361–74.

Patterson, W. D., 'Bullfight', *Saturday Review* (13 January 1968), 105.

Pearce, Richard, 'Norman Mailer's *Why Are We in Vietnam?*: A Radical Critique of Frontier Values', *Modern Fiction Studies*, 17 (Autumn 1971), 409–14.

Poirier, Richard, 'Mailer Good Form and Bad', *Saturday Review* (22 April 1972), 42–6.

Rahv, Philip, 'Crime Without Punishment', *The New York Review of Books* (20 April 1967), 14–16.

Richler, Mordecai, 'Norman Mailer', *Encounter*, 25 (July 1965), 61–4.

Rodman, Seldon, Review of *Deaths for the Ladies (and other disasters)*, *The New York Times Book Review* (8 July 1962), 7.

Sale, Roger, 'Watchman, What of the Night?', *The New York Review of Books* (6 May 1971), 13–17.

Sisk, John P., 'Aquarius Rising', *Commentary* (May 1971), 83–4.

Solotaroff, Robert, 'The Glop of the Wad', *Nation* (15 January 1973), 87–9.

Stade, George, 'Mailer and Miller', *Partisan Review*, 44, No. 4 (1977), 616–24.

Stark, John, '*Barbary Shore*: The Basis of Mailer's Best Work', *Modern Fiction Studies*, 17 (Autumn 1971), 403–8.

Tanner, Tony, 'The Great American Nightmare', *Spectator* (29 April 1966), 530–1.

Taylor, Gordon O., 'Of Adams and Aquarius', *American Literature*, 46 (March 1974), 68–82.

Toback, James, 'Norman Mailer Today', *Commentary* (October (1967), 68–76.

Trachtenberg, Alan, 'Mailer on the Steps of the Pentagon', *Nation* (27 May 1968), 701–2.

Weber, Brom, 'A Fear of Dying: Norman Mailer's *An American Dream*', *Hollins Critic*, 7 (June 1965), 1–6, 8–11.

Werge, Thomas, 'An Apocalyptic Voyage: God, Satan, and the American Tradition in Norman Mailer's *Of a Fire on the Moon*', *Review of Politics*, 34 (October 1972), 108–28.

Wills, Gary, 'Art of Not Writing Novels', *National Review* (14 January 1964), 31–3.

Wills, Gary, Review of *St George and the Godfather*, *The New York Times Book Review* (15 October 1972), 1, 22.

Wood, Michael, 'Kissing Hitler', *The New York Review of Books* (20 September 1973), 22–4.

Woodley, R., 'Literary Ticket for the 51st State', *Life* (30 May 1969), 71–2.

GENERAL MATERIAL

Books

Allen, Walter, *The Urgent West: An Introduction to the Idea of the United States* (London: John Baker, 1969).

Bergonzi, Bernard, ed., *Innovations: Essays on Art and Ideas* (London: Macmillan Press, 1968).

Calderwood, James L. and Toliver, Harold E., eds., *Perspectives on Fiction* (New York: Oxford University Press, 1968).

Davis, Robert Murray, *The Novel: Modern Essays in Criticism* (New Jersey: Prentice-Hall, 1969).

Fiedler, Leslie A., *An End to Innocence: Essays on Culture and Politics* (Boston: The Beacon Press, 1948).

Fiedler, Leslie A., *The Return of the Vanishing American* (London: Jonathan Cape, 1968).

Frye, Northrop, *Anatomy of Criticism: Four Essays* (Princeton: Princeton University Press, 1957).

Frye, Northrop, *The Critical Path: An Essay on the Social Context of Literary Criticism* (Bloomington: Indiana University Press, 1971).

Gasset, Ortega Y., *The Dehumanization of Art* (Princeton: Princeton University Press, 1968).

Guetti, James, *The Limits of Metaphor* (Ithaca: Cornell University Press, 1969).

Gold, H., ed., *Fiction of the Fifties: A Decade of American Writing* (New York: Doubleday and Company, Inc., 1959).

Hassan, Ihab, *The Literature of Silence: Henry Miller and Samuel Beckett* (New York: Alfred A. Knopf, 1967).

Hoffman, Frederick J., *The Modern Novel in America* (Chicago: Regnery Press, 1951).

Hoffman, Frederick J., *The Immortal No: Death and the Modern Imagination* (Princeton: Princeton University Press, 1964).

Hough, Graham, *Literature and Morals in the Culture of Today* (London: Duckworth, 1963).

Howe, Irving, *Politics and the Novel* (New York: The World Publishing Company, 1962).

Howe, Irving, *Decline of the New* (New York: Harcourt, Brace and World, 1970).

Klein, Marcus, *After Alienation: American Novels in Mid-Century* (New

York: The World Publishing Company, 1964).

Lukacs, Georg, *The Meaning of Contemporary Realism*, translated by John and Necke Mander (London: Merlin Press, 1963).

Marcuse, Herbert, *Eros and Civilization: A Philosophical Inquiry into Freud* (London: Routledge and Kegan Paul, 1956).

Marx, Leo, *The Machine in the Garden: Technology and the Pastoral Ideal in America* (New York: Oxford University Press, 1967).

Miller, Henry, *The Tropic of Cancer* (Paris: The Obelisk Press, 1934).

Millgate, Michael, *American Social Fiction: James to Cozzens* (Edinburgh: Oliver and Boyd, 1964).

Mizener, Arthur, *The Sense of Life in the Modern Novel* (London: Heinemann Press, 1963).

Moore, Harry T., ed., *Contemporary American Novelists* (Carbondale: Illinois University Press, 1964).

McLuhan, Marshall, *Understanding Media: The Extensions of Man* (London: Routledge and Kegan Paul, 1964).

Panichas, George A., *The Politics of Twentieth-Century Novelists* (New York: Hawthorn Books, Inc., 1971).

Podhoretz, Norman, *Making It* (New York: Random House, 1967).

Poirier, Richard, *A World Elsewhere: The Place of Style in American Literature* (London: Chatto and Windus, 1967).

Roszak, Theodore, ed., *The Making of a Counter Culture; reflections on the technocratic society and its youthful opposition* (New York: Doubleday and Company, Inc., 1969).

Sontag, Susan, *Against Interpretation* (London: Eyre and Spottiswoode, 1967).

Steiner, George, *Language and Silence* (London: Faber and Faber, 1958).

Waldmeir, Joseph J., *Recent American Fiction: Some Critical Views* (Boston: Houghton Mifflin Company, 1963).

Weinberg, Helen, *The New Novel in America: The Kafkan Mode in Contemporary Fiction* (Ithaca: Cornell University Press, 1970).

Articles

Compton, Neil, 'The Paradox of Marshall McLuhan', *New American Review*, 2, 77–94.

Glicksberg, Charles I., 'Sex in Contemporary Literature', *Colorado Quarterly* 9(Winter 1961), 277–87.

Hassan, Ihab, 'Beyond a Theory of Literature: Intimations of

Apocalypse?', *Comparative Literature Studies*, 1, No. 4, (1964), 261–71.

Kazin, Alfred, 'The Alone Generation', *Harpers Magazine*, 219 (October 1959), 127–31.

MacDonald, Dwight, 'The Bright Young Men In The Arts', *Esquire*, 50 (September 1958), 38–40.

Philips, William, 'Writing About Sex', *Partisan Review*, 24 (Fall 1967), 552–63.

Spender, Stephen, 'Writers and Politics', *Partisan Review*, 34 (Summer 1967), 359–81.

Index